The Uncultured Wars

The Uncultured Wars

Arabs, Muslims, and the
Poverty of Liberal Thought

NEW ESSAYS

Steven Salaita

ZED BOOKS

London & New York

To the unheard victims of altruism

*The Uncultured Wars: Arabs, Muslims, and the Poverty
of Liberal Thought – New Essays* was first published in 2008 by
Zed Books Ltd, 7 Cynthia Street, London N1 9JF, UK and
Room 400, 175 Fifth Avenue, New York, NY 10010, USA

www.zedbooks.co.uk

Designed and typeset by illuminati, Grosmont, www.illuminatibooks.co.uk
Cover designed by Rogue Four Design
Printed and bound in Malta by Gutenberg Press Ltd

Distributed in the USA exclusively by Palgrave Macmillan,
a division of St Martin's Press, LLC,
175 Fifth Avenue, New York, NY 10010, USA

A catalogue record for this book is available from the British Library
Library of Congress Cataloging in Publication Data available

ISBN 978 1 84813 234 4 Hb
ISBN 978 1 84813 235 1 Pb
ISBN 978 1 84813 236 8 Eb

Contents

Acknowledgements

I have been blessed with a set of friends and mentors (usually both at once) whose support enables me to write in the way that I do and about the things I examine. This book was written during a difficult personal time, and it never would have been finished without my friends/mentors, who continue to love and support me despite the fact that I never answer the phone.

An effusive metaphorical bear hug, then, to those kind enough to have offered feedback: Mohammed Abed, an intellectual ally and brilliant moral analyst; Evelyn Azeeza Alsultany, who is expertly saving Arabs and Muslims from the drudges of academic colonization; Rima Najjar Kapitan, a dear friend whose dedication to justice has never allowed my own to lag; and Deborah Alkamano, fellow traveler, all-around inspiration, older sister.

I would also like to thank my wonderful colleagues in the English Department at Virginia Tech, particularly Virginia

Fowler, whose reading of this book in manuscript form was remarkably helpful. My students, both undergraduate and graduate, have furnished my life with a constant intellectual richness. I appreciate their astute insights and lively counter-arguments, which have played a significant role in the way I have developed the material in this book. Ellen McKinlay's constant professionalism is likewise appreciated.

There is no way I can express adequately what I would like to say to Michael and Danya, so I will leave it at this: I owe to you all the words on these pages. My parents, Nasr and Miriam, have supported my pursuits and career choices without fail, and for that, and so many other things, I express to them my love.

Last and most important, no work of mine could ever be complete without the encouragement and keen critical eye of Diana, the most intelligent social critic I have yet encountered. Thank you for this life, a by-product of your ambition.

Introduction

These wars today are brutal, baleful, ubiquitous. They are rhetorical and military. They are political and cultural. They are individual and international. They are local and universal. They are perpetually incongruous. But they have something in common: they are all uncultured.

An absence of culture, of course, is construed in the Western imagination as barbarity. This construal is possible through an attenuated notion of culture as something that refined people travel to encounter rather than something that is lived as an unspoken realness in the minutiae of daily life.

To be uncultured these days isn't merely to be unrefined. It is to be complicit somehow in the grand topic of our age, terrorism. Identifying terrorism is the sort of act that alters jurisprudence and influences policy and so it is necessarily tendentious. It is also a racialized act. Arabs and Muslims have become in certain ways coterminous with terrorism. We are thus quintessentially uncultured.

I embrace my uncultured existence. In the morality plays that increasingly define American rhetoric, I cannot escape being relegated to the encroaching corpus of premodernity. In the clash of civilizations I exist somewhere There. I am an American-born alien, the new domestic foreigner. I embrace being uncultured, though, because to be cultured is to have been corrupted through filtering, purification, or distillation.

I have already lost the culture wars, and so with this collection I zestfully enter into the uncultured wars. I have wanted for a while to engage some of the issues that occupy the chattering and intellectual classes in today's United States. Rather than engaging those issues through various op-eds or a monograph, I decided that the genre of essay is the perfect medium to fulfill my proclivity.

An essay is eternally versatile: it can do and look like almost anything. An essay can cover any length, from the minimalist to the exhaustive. It can be prudent or cantankerous, often simultaneously. It can be stunningly revealing or majestically impersonal. It is a fun and rewarding genre, but not an easy one. It takes time and practice to develop the skills to make an essay work, even if it first seems that the genre represents little more than literate people sharing thoughts or imparting opinion. We shouldn't confuse people like Thomas Friedman with essayists, a class that includes folks like Arundhati Roy, Virginia Woolf, Gore Vidal, Matt Taibbi, Ahdaf Soueif, Stanley Crouch, Winona LaDuke, bell hooks, and Taiaiake Alfred, essayists with whom

I don't always agree but who represent the genre with passion and skill. Producing nonfiction prose that imparts an opinion is one thing. Writing an essay, though, requires the presence of artistry; and if an essay is to be good then it needs to rearrange some type of orthodoxy. That's why most newspaper columnists are corporate exhibitionists, not essayists. Or, to be fair, most of them are simply bad essayists.

The essay has a wonderful history in the Arab American literary tradition. One of the best known Arab American writers, Edward Said, was a prolific essayist; even much of his scholarship has the feel and tone of an essay. Well before Said, however, members of *al-Muhjar* published topical and stimulating essays; these writers included Ameen Rihani, Gibran Khalil Gibran, and Mikhail Naimy. Today's Arab American essayists – Joseph Massad, Noami Shihab Nye, Joanna Kadi, Diana Abu-Jaber, Lisa Suhair Majaj, Gregory Orfalea, Ray Hanania, Evelyn Azeeza Alsultany, Elmaz Abinader, and the many others I am surely forgetting – represent the genre with a diversity of content and style emblematic of the manifold community with which they identify.

I will be concerned in many of these essays with morality, a term whose potential for ambiguity or acrimony cannot be underestimated. I would like to take a moment, then, to clarify its usage in the pieces that follow. I adhere to a specific notion of morality, as distinct from moralism, which is an expression of sanctimony. I employ morality as being coterminous with a committed accountability to comprehensive human wellness – socially, economically, ecologically, and politically. I'm not enamored of the word *responsibility*, but I have in mind something comparable when I invoke matters that I conceptualize as being fundamentally moral – perhaps *answerability* is a better choice. I want people – myself foremost among them – to be answerable to the multiple consequences of the choices they make as consumers, spectators, and political agents. To be aware of consequences that require serious analysis to discover is the hallmark of a healthy morality. Essays can challenge us to undertake this sort of discovery.

My favorite form is the political essay, which accounts for the majority of the pieces in this collection. I would love for more Arab American writers, especially the growing class of emerging authors, to take up the genre. Not only is essay writing stimulating and sometimes cathartic, it's yet another way for us, as Arab Americans, to continue speaking on our own behalf. We will end up presenting vastly different visions, but whichever vision each of us wishes to express, at least those visions will be ours.

And if you have picked up this book, whatever your background, these essays have become yours. Do with them what you wish. But please don't call them cultured.

Anti-Arab racism, American liberals, and the new civilian terrorists

In July 2006, when a Hizbullah squadron entered into northern Israel and abducted two soldiers, killing eight others, American print and visual media reflexively described the move as an act of terrorism and deemed Hizbullah a 'terrorist organization.' The descriptors assumed a particular urgency because they created a pretext for Israel to undertake a heavy bombing campaign of Lebanon, resulting in much death and destruction. The many Lebanese and Palestinian civilian deaths would also come to be justified by Israel's purported battle against terrorism.

Media on both the right and the left accepted Israel and the United States' description of Hizbullah as a terrorist organization, but the veracity of that description should have been questioned. The immorality of Israel's wanton destruction does not present much of a political or ethical debate for those who would distinguish between military targets and civilian ones, or between terrorists and ordinary people. The problem is that American media repeatedly omitted either distinction, thereby transforming Israel's aggression into an act of self-defense. Such omissions were plausible because of a profound anti-Arab racism in the United States that inspires the dehumanization of Arabs and reduces complex social and cultural phenomena in the Arab World to the level of irrational barbarism.

Had commentators and audiences spent time exploring those phenomena rather than unthinkingly describing Hizbullah as terroristic, the boundaries of debate might have shifted in productive ways. Hizbullah has engaged in acts of terrorism, the most notorious being the 1983 bombing of the Marine barracks in Beirut, but its role in Lebanon has long been more complex than that of an armed militia. It also is a legitimate political organization with a solid base of support and provides necessary social services to the Shi'a of Lebanon, the nation's poorest demographic aside from the non-citizen Palestinian refugees. Hizbullah also has cultural appeal in parts of Lebanon because it emphasizes the indigineity of its world-view by conceptualizing itself as the rightful purveyor of a native voice as against the interference of foreign powers. The organization, though, is armed and during its history has undertaken operations that can rightly be described as terrorist. This is merely one dimension of a complex mission, but it is the dimension that has come to define Hizbullah in the American imagination.

In fact, according to American media all Arab violence is terrorism. These media never delineate which criteria produce such a judgment, most likely because the criteria are only perfunctory suppositions inspired by the racist impulse to assume that Arabs never have good reason to commit violence and are thus irrational, while Americans would never be irrational enough to commit violence without good reason. The suppositions are de-contextualized from relevant historical details – for example, Israel's abduction of Lebanese citizens – and are conceptualized as neutral judgments that arise from objective reasoning.

Leaving aside the issue of whether objectivity ever is possible (it is not), the supposedly neutral judgments about what constitutes terrorism reveal much about how anti-Arab racism functions implicitly and explicitly in the United States. Condemnation of terrorism seems on the surface to be a neutral act; after all, who would argue that terrorism is a good thing? In fact, however, collapsing and equating all Arab violence as 'acts of terrorism' reveals that the condemnation of terrorism is grounded in politicized tendencies that reinforce the erstwhile precepts of white supremacy. Why, for example, are American commentators so certain that Hizbullah is a terrorist organization but withhold that designation from, say, American soldiers who commit atrocities (Abu Ghraib, Haditha) or Israeli settlers in the West Bank, who squat on stolen land and organize mobs to murder Palestinian civilians?

This question is not rhetorical. If we endeavor to provide an answer, we will encounter the American tradition of dehumanizing its geopolitical enemies, in this case by totalizing as terrorists Arabs who contravene the United States' imperial ambitions. Underlying this totalization is the assumption that

Arabs are incapable of entering into modernity and that whatever demands they express through violence are necessarily reasonless whereas American violence, however ugly, always intends to serve the interests of progress. The historical record indicates that this formulation has been utilized to great effect in the American polity ever since the time of slave rebellions and the genocide of North America's indigenous populations.

The flippancy with which American media apply the word 'terrorism' to Arab populations likewise reinforces the notion that violence in the Arab World is ahistorical and therefore senseless. Arabs in turn become a people without narratives who belong to a culture incapable of rationality. These perceptions skew Americans' understanding of both the United States and the Arab World.

If, for instance, the abduction by Hizbullah of two Israeli soldiers was so confidently designated an act of terrorism, then it would appear that the operable criterion for defining terrorism – a violent action against an enemy army – is one that exemplifies the whole of American military history. Indeed, this criterion would render all militaries agents of terrorism (a point some pacifists would argue), but in this instance media applied it selectively to Hizbullah in order to validate an extant belief that its violence lacks purpose. (It has purpose, which is not to say that we must accept that purpose morally or politically.) When Americans acknowledge a purpose to Arab violence, they attribute it to religious or cultural rather than to political factors, which is to tacitly assign it the status of an inborn characteristic.

In July 2006, when Israel's destruction of Lebanon had accelerated, a variation of this discourse began to emerge: the notion that one cannot rightly distinguish between terrorists and civilians because most of the civilians in Lebanon were either in cahoots or in sympathy with Hizbullah. Zionists have periodically used such a rationale to mystify Israel's ethnic cleansing of Palestinians in the Occupied Territories. American officials also have employed the same rationale to justify the mounting civilian deaths in Iraq. But at no time has the rationale become so inscribed in mainstream commentary as during Israel's war on the Lebanese people.

Perhaps the exemplar of this perspective is Alan Dershowitz, the famed Harvard civil libertarian. In an op-ed published in the *Los Angeles Times*, Dershowitz dismisses Israel's brutality, asking, 'But just who is a "civilian" in the age of terrorism, when militants don't wear uniforms, don't belong to regular armies and easily blend into civilian populations?' The implication of this question is clear: all Lebanese people are potential terrorists and are therefore worthy of slaughter without Israeli or American culpability. Dershowitz perfumes this malevolent argument with cumbersome jargon, introducing his concept of 'the continuum of civilianity,' which is a fancy way of saying that Israel cannot act immorally against a population devoid of fundamental morality. Dershowitz, who implies that dead Lebanese civilians are complicit in their own deaths, synthesizes his argument in the article's final sentence: 'Every civilian death is a tragedy, but some are more tragic than others.'

Dershowitz's abhorrent moral formulation resulted from Lebanon's mounting civilian death toll and the diminishing number of Israeli casualties, which initially dominated news coverage. The ensuing shift in coverage was supplemented by a plethora of damning images circulated among alternative media, including pictures of Israeli children writing messages on soon-to-be-launched missiles, and charred and dismembered Arab children. Once Israel's targeting of civilians could no longer be denied, Dershowitz had to find a way to alter his rhetorical approach while remaining committed to Israel. He had long argued that Israel never targets civilians, but once that claim was disproved by the same media that could always be counted on to uphold it, he decided to argue instead that the civilians Israel was slaughtering weren't *really* civilians, an argument whose sole evidence was Dershowitz's opinion.

Dershowitz's op-ed is an example of anti-Arab racism because to assign sympathies to an entire people, whether those sympathies are flattering or demeaning, is to immure them to something of an ethnic spectacle that eradicates their agency. Moreover, the notion that all Lebanese are potential terrorists is completely indemonstrable and therefore an unjustifiable totalization. The argument reinforces a belief among most Zionists that aggression is endemic to Arabs and alien to Jews and white Americans.

Dershowitz may be the exemplar of this sort of argument, but he certainly is not its only advocate. After Israel's invasion, neoconservative media – on other issues enemies of the liberal

Dershowitz – reactively blamed the imbroglio on Hizbullah (and Syria and Iran, the organization's financial sponsors and the scapegoats of neoconservative ideology). This blame was replete with the racist invective typical of neoconservative commentators, which has included calling Middle Easterners 'ragheads,' claiming that all Palestinians look like rats and have beady eyes, disparaging people with 'fan belts' and 'diapers' on their heads, and suggesting that the United States strike Mecca with nuclear weapons. (See my *Anti-Arab Racism in the USA* for extensive examples of neoconservative racism.)

The more noteworthy responses to the invasion arose from liberal and in some cases progressive analysts, who eschewed overt racism but allowed dogma about Arab barbarity to influence their analyses. An editorial in *The Nation*, for example, expressed an anti-war position but did so by assessing strategic implications rather than human traumas, exemplified by the article's synopsis on the front page of the magazine's website: '[T]he spreading violence in Lebanon and Gaza demonstrates that the collective punishment of the Palestinian and Lebanese people will only further radicalize the region.' This perspective mentions nothing of the immorality of Israel's collective punishment, emphasizing instead its dangers to the West and ignoring the scores of dead Arab civilians.

Only once in the editorial does *The Nation* offer moral condemnation, in the singular appearance of the word 'inhumane.' Otherwise, it recycles the canard that the Near East is populated not by civilians but by radicals perpetually on the brink of becoming even more radicalized. I would not judge this editorial to be racist, but find it disappointing that a venerable journal of progressive opinion in the United States failed to humanize what at that point had become a severely degraded population.

The *New York Times* recycled the same canard in an editorial in which it claimed that 'more civilian deaths in Lebanon won't make Israel safer.' A diligent reader might ask why the *Times* didn't suggest that more civilian deaths in Lebanon would be morally repugnant or a continued breach of international law. Ardent emphasis on strategy in the face of slaughter is only possible through a dehumanization shared by writer and audience. Monitoring corporate print media in the month following Israel's assault of Lebanon, I found no commentary that examined Hizbullah's strategy without also condemning or at least noting the immorality of targeting Israeli civilians, a result of the fact that Israeli Jews are securely humanized in the United States.

Another dubious leftist commentary appeared in *The Progressive*, where Ruth Conniff validated the false but widespread notion that while violence exists among both Arabs and Israelis, terrorism is exclusive to the Arabs. Conniff accomplished this validation through her unimaginative diction, assigning 'terrorist violence' to Arabs and 'military reprisals' to Israel. She also observes that 'Israelis are not all gung-ho for war,' an observation that leads readers to infer that all Arabs are. As with *The Nation*, it would be unfair to judge Conniff's argument as racist, but it brings to our attention the important point that some of the anti-Arab racism generated on the right finds its way subtly to political analyses on the left.

In some cases, though, the left as represented by liberal Zionists recycles blatant anti-Arab racism, a fact evident in an op-ed published by *Washington Post* columnist Richard Cohen in July 2006. Cohen begins his analysis by making a moral distinction between Jews and Arabs: 'Israeli conscripts or reservists do not think death and martyrdom are the same thing. No virgins await Jews in heaven.' He later invokes the age-old myth that Israel is an innocent victim of Arab hostility: 'Israel is, as I have often said, unfortunately located, gentrifying a pretty bad neighborhood.' Cohen's usage here is intentionally passive and thus ambiguous, permitting him to avoid the inconvenient fact that Israel's unfortunate location is not a historical accident but the result of an intricately planned and brutally enforced colonial incursion. The ambiguity likewise enables Cohen to ignore the decisive issue of colonization and thus to reproduce the racist hypothesis that Arabs attack Israelis simply because they like to kill Jews. Of the well-documented propensity of Israeli Jews to kill Arabs Cohen is frightfully clear: 'The only way to ensure that babies don't die in their cribs and old people in the streets is to make the Lebanese or the Palestinians understand that if they, no matter how reluctantly, host those rockets, they will pay a very, very steep price.'

I have been using the early stages of Israel's destruction of Lebanon as a test case for the pervasiveness of anti-Arab racism because this racism, albeit continuous, tends like all types of racism to intensify when geopolitics necessitate its existence. This reality would be impossible if it weren't already an available discourse and if it weren't such an effective way to rationalize Israeli and American truculence in the Arab World and to justify the post-9/11 governmental assault on constitutional rights and civil liberties (see further David Cole, *Enemy Aliens*; and Elaine Hagopian, ed., *Civil Rights in Peril*).

The most conspicuous example of institutionalized anti-Arab racism during the early stages of Israel's destruction was a nonbinding resolution blaming Arabs for the violence, which Congress passed on a vote of 410:8, a rare show of bipartisanship (support for Israel and for corporate greed are the only issues in the US government that consistently inspire bipartisanship). John McCain, typifying the propensity of American politicians to rationalize the murder of Arab civilians, announced that if Hizbullah is 'going to launch attacks from the Lebanese territory, then tragically the Lebanese government and people pay a price for that.' By McCain's reasoning, Palestinians would be justified in killing American civilians because Israel regularly launches attacks on them with weaponry provided by the United States. (For the record, I do not believe that Palestinians have a moral right to commit violence against American civilians, but I do believe that they have more of a moral claim to the use of such violence than do Israelis vis-à-vis Arabs. This is so based on their position as a justifiably aggrieved party.)

Anti-Arab racism isn't merely intertwined with American and Israeli atrocities. It has had a consistent presence in the United States for over a century and its modern incarnation can roughly be traced to the 1967 Arab–Israeli War. Anti-Arab racism has traditionally existed on the left as well as the right (as have all forms of racism; the American left has a long history of legitimizing the same things it claims to oppose). Post-9/11 a handful of alternative media (e.g. *International Socialist Review*, *Palestine Chronicle*, *Democracy Now!*) have either avoided simplistic analyses or have actively challenged anti-Arab racism. Still, few forums provide space for Arabs to articulate their own challenges, a problem of accessibility that continues to affect all ethnic minorities in the United States.

Liberals and progressives, on the other hand, traditionally have been weak on the issue of anti-Arab racism, not only doing too little to challenge it but in some cases reproducing it. We can go back to another piece by Ruth Conniff for a relevant example, shifting our attention to Iraq. Conniff writes,

> A neighbor of mine, back on a short leave from an 18-month tour as a National Guardsman in Iraq, expressed disgust with the Iraqis, describing them as a backward people who don't even want our help to build schools. They prefer that their kids remain ignorant, and work on the farm, he said. That alienated feeling is mutual, as Iraqis view the United States with increasing anger. It's not a hopeful atmosphere.

Unlike the other Conniff piece I discussed, I would deem this one racist. We can, first of all, identify the guardsman she quotes – presuming that she imparts his comments accurately – as an anti-Arab racist, given that he totalizes Iraqis as backward, petulant, ungrateful, and ignorant. That he spent time at war in Iraq and likely encountered trauma there are irrelevant to my judging him as racist, because I don't find in those facts plausible excuses for negative totalization; the notion that American soldiers are allowed to degrade the people in the countries they invade is malicious and only perpetuates American military brutality.

We needn't conflate Conniff with the soldier in order to identify her own racism. She articulates it herself through her framing of his comments and in her response to them. Describing his blatant racism with forlorn sympathy as an 'alienated feeling' is at best a nonsensical interpretation and at worst an endorsement of it. Conniff further implicates herself by noting that the 'alienated feeling is mutual,' a claim for which she presents no evidence (because there is none to support such an exaggerated generalization). The claim acts as a sleight of hand: she absolves the soldier of his bigoted attitude by presuming that Iraqis, the silent party in her article, must likewise harbor bigoted attitudes. Conniff could have used the occasion of the soldier's comments to point out that war fosters racism, or that Iraqis clearly are human enough to run their own affairs without the assistance of racist guardsmen, but instead she mourns his alienation as if that accounts for the unwillingness of Iraqis to submit themselves to American domination.

Conniff's formulation is reminiscent of a 2002 piece by Barbara Ehrenreich, who gained some notoriety in 2005 for allegedly calling Sudanese Arabs 'guys riding around on camels.' The piece, supportive of the war on Afghanistan but critical of the approaching invasion of Iraq, argues, as do so many other articles by progressives, for strategic rather than moral or legal probity. If the US invades Iraq, Ehrenreich fears, 'a generation of young Muslims in Riyadh or Cairo or Hamburg will seek martyrdom by taking out some of us.' Rather than inventing a phantom threat, Ehrenreich might have noted the harsh illegality of taking out some of 'them.' Strategy, of course, is an important consideration, but exclusive discussion of it at the expense of human concerns ultimately manufactures dehumanization.

More damningly, Ehrenreich employs the words 'terror' and 'terrorist' with uncritical certainty, writing, 'With great reluctance and foreboding, I had to agree with the Bush Administration that America needed to launch a "war on terror," or at least a determined effort to apprehend the terrorists.' Here Ehrenreich confines terrorism to the Islamic World, assuming that America engages in legitimate forms of violence and thus recapitulating the tired formulation that 'a whole world, that of Islam,' enjoys killing Westerners for reasons external to geopolitics. Take, for instance, her unctuous condemnation of Afghan civilian deaths: 'Unknown numbers of civilians – somewhere between 500 and 3000 – managed to get in the way of the bombs and the bullets, earning us the lasting enmity of their survivors.'

As with other examples of tacit racism on the left, Ehrenreich's is articulated through a curious sentence structure, in this case one implying that Afghans actively tried to get themselves killed by American weaponry; she ignores the demonstrable possibility that the American weaponry managed to find the Afghan civilians by design. Progressive anti-Arab racism, then, is much more subtle than that on the right, which often is blatant and thus readily detectable. On the left, though, it sometimes can be found in what writers assert through omission when they are selectively descriptive and what they say implicitly about the value of Arab and Muslim peoples when they choose to emphasize the sanctity of American life.

Hence the most consistent feature of anti-Arab racism in the United States: the incessant equation of Arabs with ruthless, innate violence devoid of the context invariably granted every instance of American or Israeli aggression. There is a self-aggrandizement in the United States around the issue of terrorism, one that claims to be neutral but is always political and one that rationalizes domestic and international depravity through emotional manipulation. The progressive left will never forge a productive resistance as long as it continues to tacitly embolden this self-aggrandizement rather than identifying and interrogating it.

Another related problem of the liberal left around the issue of anti-Arab racism is an unwillingness to engage Arabs on the basis of their fundamental humanity. It has been well established among people of color that racism cannot take root in any society without liberal acquiescence. Liberalism confounds the problem by providing its advocates with a comforting illusion that the fact of being liberal is enough to identify as anti-racist.

Nobody has the right to identify as anti-racist based merely on ideology, nor does one have the right to that identification based on having Arab friends, anti-war yard signs, 'coexist' bumper stickers, Darwin fishes, co-op memberships, or good intentions. Being anti-racist – being truly opposed to racism – requires more than sloganeering and more than assuming the superficial markings of a certain political ideology. Being anti-racist means being willing to sacrifice privilege to the benefit of all humans. It means a desire to act rather than to philosophize. It means an eagerness to learn about others rather than an inclination to lecture to them. It means constantly seeking one's own complicity in the very things one abhors.

It means all of these things because of how deeply ingrained racism is in the United States. One doesn't end racism merely by collecting a few minority friends or plopping down an anti-war yard sign. To end racism in the United States, we would need to challenge all that is considered fundamentally American because the version of Americanness with which we're confronted today relies profoundly on the existence of racism, including anti-Arab racism, which underlies much of the United States' late-capitalist geopolitics.

We should therefore do away with the notion that liberalism automatically equates to tolerance or that liberals are dedicated anti-racists. Liberals are, and long have been, part of the same system that created the racism under discussion in this essay. This valorization of tolerance, which has been put to extended use for a long time by American liberals, is the material articulation of refusing to confront Arabs on the basis of their fundamental humanity. The admiration of liberals for this seemingly inclusive concept reflects their unwillingness to undertake what is necessary to eliminate racism.

Tolerance in fact is a stupid concept and a pernicious goal that likes to pretend it nurtures egalitarianism. Tolerance as an organizing principle against racism or any other form of social injustice is pernicious because it does little more than reinforce whatever injustice it ostensibly sets out to eliminate. Dutiful advocates of tolerance probably feel that their ethics of toleration are both noble and useful. But I'm hesitant to let the matter rest at this speculation. Surely there are a number of liberals who know very well that tolerance is a smokescreen that effectively precludes actual egalitarianism and merely consolidates the white superstructure that has governed North America since the early sixteenth century. Tolerance stops short of action; it never demands that people reorganize the unjust political mechanisms that produce racism and from which its beneficiaries, including the majority of white liberals, derive socio-economic and emotional privileges.

Besides, my goals as an individual belonging to a minority community are manifold and ambitious; being 'tolerated' is not one of them. I would much prefer – as would my 'ethnic' brethren, I dare say – being respected on the merits of my inherent humanity and having access to the social rights and responsibilities that accrue from subsisting within a system of true social equality. Both American and international law, in any case, dictate that I have rights beyond the supposed munificence of being tolerated. To be tolerated is inevitably to be subordinate to those with the power to deem me tolerable – and thus intolerable should my fortunes change.

The liberal shibboleth of tolerance has been common in the United States post-9/11, particularly in relation to Arabs and Arab Americans. Arabs generally are to be avoided, despised, incarcerated. In moments of generosity, however, the Arab is transformed in the liberal imagination from alien presence into tolerable object of curiosity, an object that ends up validating the almost messianic righteousness inscribed in that liberal imagination. Because Arabs have been subject to the competing (but not necessarily antagonistic) strategies of castigation (among conservatives) and toleration (among liberals), they have been marked as different. And in this conceptualization of Arabs as somehow apart from the rest of Americans, as slightly different in generous analyses and as hideously savage in less pretentious ones, the mythology of race continues to be decisive in the United States.

This mythology, albeit consistent, emerged upon Israel's invasion of Lebanon, as it does when any geopolitical moment renders it expedient. It enables liberals and progressives to be sufficiently critical of the United States and Israel while upholding the longstanding assumptions that relegate Arabs to the status of subhuman – and that, more important, safeguard white privilege in the face of what true responsibility would necessitate. The fact that white liberals so infrequently embrace true responsibility is enough to question their ultimate loyalties, which, when not in actual support of American and Israeli imperialism, are unknowingly in collusion with them. This support and collusion, masquerading as enlightenment, only exists because of the simultaneous but never accidental presence of anti-Arab racism.

The indispensably expendable

During the summer of 2006, John Nichols, opinion editor of the progressive *Madison Capital Times* and staff writer for *The Nation*, appeared on Radio 1670, The Pulse, to discuss a piece he had written about Israel's invasion of Lebanon. His interviewer was John Sylvester, aka Sly, best known around southern Wisconsin for once calling Condoleezza Rice 'Aunt Jemina' and Colin Powell an 'Uncle Tom.'

Sly, a dedicated liberal, is staunchly Zionist, and wanted to take issue with Nichols's supposed criticism of Israel. Here is what Nichols had written:

[N]o genuine friend of Israel can be happy with what is being done in that country's name by Prime Minister Ehud Olmert and his misguided followers.

Israel's attack on Lebanon, which has already killed and wounded hundreds and destroyed much of that fragile democracy's infrastructure – including airports, seaports, bridges and roads – has done nothing to make Israel safer or more secure from threats posed by the militant Islamic organization Hezbollah. Indeed, the terrorist group's attacks on targets in northern Israel have become more brazen – and deadly – since Israel began striking Lebanon.

No serious participant in the contemporary discourse would deny that Israel has a right to protect itself. But no one in their right mind thinks Israel is going about the mission in a smart manner.

Like contemporary liberalist calls for the United States to withdraw its troops from Iraq, Nichols's analysis reinforces Israel's right to violence and then encourages it not to terminate its attacks but to practice a wiser form of aggressiveness. Nichols is correct that as a nation-state Israel has a right to protect itself. However, in professing the obvious he overlooks a number of crucial particulars. A more intelligent analysis might ask why Israel's protection is treated as an intuitive moral proposition. By particularizing intuition, this sort of moral proposition renders the Arabs inhuman because it abrogates their right to be protected from Israel. That is to say, Nichols can assert his commonsensical argument only at the expense of the Lebanese. He might find a perusal of Antonio Gramsci useful.

That the Zionist Sly took issue with an argument that essentially affirmed or tacitly rationalized all of Israel's brutality is something of a curiosity. Sly's reaction illuminates the devotion of Zionists to complete obedience but is useful to folks like Nichols, who can then pretend to be intellectually sovereign or oppositional. It's merely a different way of sacrificing himself for Israel.

During the program, Sly and Nichols had little to argue over. Israel, Nichols announced, exhibiting the sort of oppositional stance for which privileged whites are famous, is in 'unfair circumstances.' His appearance on The Pulse lasted twenty-two minutes. In those twenty-two minutes Nichols managed to say not a single humanizing thing about the Palestinians or Arabs. Instead, he called some of them 'crazy terrorists' and others of them 'sophisticated terrorists.' He also noted that 'there are a lot of bad people there [in the Middle East], with all due respect,' a disclaimer that nobody has ever confused with a respectful act. What has happened to Israel, on the other hand, is 'terrible' and 'awful' because Israel has 'been forced into that situation.' Nichols expressed profound concern for Israel's security while ignoring the right of Palestinians to the same. (Indeed, as the colonized party, their right to security is even more immediate than Israel's.) The only potentially humanizing thing he managed to say about Arabs is 'there are a lot of Arabs who are frankly not crazy and are very responsible,' a formulation that frankly led listeners to infer that the majority of Arabs are insane and irresponsible.

Nichols's argument personifies vigilant inanity. He's an invention of the liberal imagination, a gimmick summoned into existence because centers of power welcome – nay, require – the sort of resistance he proffers.

At one point in the program, Sly speculated that a continued Saddam Hussein dictatorship would have been better for the United States. Nichols agreed, suggesting that 'there's no question' that with Saddam in place the region would be better for 'us.'

Nichols's colleague and editor, Katrina vanden Heuvel, is fond of professing a comparable sentiment in the form of a slogan: 'What's bad for the nation is good for *The Nation*.' Vanden Heuvel deploys this slogan as a comedic device in public appearances and as something of a revelatory pun or critical witticism on *The Nation*'s website. In fact, the slogan is vigilantly inane, intimating either an absence of analytical ability or ethical depravity. (And the rest of the world, I suppose, can sit around waiting to be included.)

Does vanden Heuvel mean to say that she would forfeit all the privileges commensurate with her position at *The Nation* if only the nation would become good? In other words, why doesn't she use the following slogan: What's good for the nation is bad for those *The Nation* claims to oppose.

In the first year of my current faculty position I was invited to a party in honor of the department's distinguished alumni – *distinguished*, of course, being a euphemism for *rich*. Given that the alumni were graduates of an English program in addition to being rich, it wasn't much of a surprise that they were all white. With two exceptions, me and a black woman, the approximately twenty faculty present also were white. The black woman left early because of a prior commitment.

The four-person catering staff, adorned in white double-ply jackets, were all black. With its black waiting staff in bleached costume and white patrons cupping wine chalices, the party resembled a scene from the Old South.

I have never been considered white by my peers and have never considered myself white, but I'm light-skinned enough to achieve a social invisibility when interacting with whites, who imagine me sympathetic enough to let me in on the secret. Anybody who has spent time in all-white spaces knows exactly what 'the secret' is. Along with Israel's nuclear weapons, though, this happens to be the world's worst kept secret, one that African Americans themselves know quite well. It is a secret, then, only in the sense that its white purveyors insist that it doesn't exist.

The secret is that in social spaces devoid of black participants, racism becomes de rigueur. Outright hostility is acceptable, but snide comments or subtle loathing will do. This party, then, functioned as a veritable safe zone for white supremacy (though it should be noted that an absence of black bodies certainly isn't necessary to the articulation of white racism).

It didn't take long for the elegant guests to begin complaining about the black faculty caucus, concluding that 'with them, something is always amiss.'

Conversation shifted inevitably to the religious right, a favored topic among liberal academic windbags. (Invoking and then savaging conspicuously odious people in order to profess righteousness without actually interrogating privilege is a specialty of the professoriate.)

Amid the rehearsed complaints about overweight theocrats and black people who exhibit agency, a faculty member joined the conversation. 'Do I hear you speaking about Jerry Falwell?'

Upon our affirmation, he remarked, 'All would be right in the world if he got caught in a hotel room with a black boy.'

The person who made this remark wasn't John Nichols or Katrina vanden Heuvel, although, from a moral standpoint, he may as well have been. All three speakers utilize the same assumptions in producing what they imagine to be a meaningful and even open-minded argument. Those arguments represent a peculiar form of white liberal rhetoric, one that projects an interest in social justice while actually functioning only to preserve the interests of white liberals. Liberalism, like all political world-views, is necessarily abstract, but here it is rendered palpable and endowed with a set of imperatives that subordinate all other forms of agency.

This rhetorical outlook is pernicious because it always requires somebody to be sacrificed. It is the disenfranchised inevitably put up for sacrifice.

Sly and Nichols, for instance, are willing to wish dictatorship on people as long as their interests as Americans are preserved. By performing callousness, this sort of attitude creates a rationale for imperialism and colonization and ultimately forms a dialectical relationship with racism. Centralizing a narrow geopolitical interest as the basis of policy analysis, Nichols fortifies a hierarchy that precludes any realistic possibility of transnational dialogue or cooperation. And he re-familiarizes the United States as a natural site of political normativity. In the process he further alienates Iraq, a place that subsequently becomes, as Nichols put it, 'too crazy.' It is easy to become indifferent to the inhabitants of this sort of place.

Vanden Heuvel's oft-repeated slogan is slightly more repellent, if only because she is prepared to sacrifice the rest of the world in addition to Iraqis. For those who might argue that none of these liberals is truly advocating any sort of sacrifice, I would suggest that the sacrifice is detectable as an implicit subtext without which their slogans and statements would forfeit meaning as either pun or comment. Take, for instance, the formulation 'what's bad for the nation is good for *The Nation*.' Vanden Heuvel is the editor of *The Nation* and thus has an interest in growing that publication. Even though in any other context vanden Heuvel would likely argue that nobody should ever be sacrificed to somebody else's benefit, when she repeats the slogan she in fact presents that argument, which then becomes a relevant barometer of her moral imperatives as a prominent liberal. She should be smart enough to know that one shouldn't pronounce slogans that do not accurately represent one's sensibilities. In any case, her choice of slogan in the first place is unmistakable evidence of concern for her own status as a devoted liberal vis-à-vis her concern for the well-being of those who experience firsthand the badness of the nation (and *The Nation*). She created that slogan, after all; it wasn't handed to her.

If anybody is still unconvinced of the slogan as metonym of crass self-interest, perhaps vanden Heuvel's former colleague David Corn, now with *Mother Jones*, can help put it in better perspective: "'I gotta pay my bills, I got a family to feed," he says. "What we say at the magazine is what's bad for the nation is good for *The Nation*."'

We don't like to think that folks who articulate lofty ideals could in reality be entrenched in the forms of power they purport to oppose. For this reason, it is easy to rationalize seemingly throwaway statements as harmless witticisms or rhetorical curiosities. I would encourage others, however, to respond the hard way, to keep sight of the fact that liberals need to be taken on just like all political movements and powerful individuals. Nobody should be beyond reproach or above challenge. This point is particularly true of those who claim most ardently to work beyond or above immorality.

We have to ask hard questions of liberals and challenge their self-made authority without apologia. Neoconservatives and other explicit racists are too easy, too obvious. By focusing on them almost exclusively we confer on them a sort of power they don't possess on their own. And it's not necessarily among these people that real power is circulated. Power welcomes the presence of opposition; it is subversion that power deplores. Never has a subversive proclamation appeared in the work of Nichols, vanden Heuvel, and Corn.

I have not forgotten the most troubling of the statements presented earlier in this essay. It warrants a climactic placement because it represents a culmination of sorts. My colleague's comment about the late Jerry Falwell doing what should be unmentionable things is the quintessence of the sort of liberalist logic evident in the discourse of *The Nation* staff. In other words, my colleague's comment is where that logic will invariably lead. It has no other place to go.

My colleague would probably justify the comment by proclaiming it actually to be a salvo for justice. Jerry Falwell is a dangerous theocrat. He is an incessant moralist. As with most moralists, he is bound to be a hypocrite, possibly even a shocking hypocrite, shocking enough to be scandalous, at which point his career might be undermined or at least compromised. Nothing would be more scandalous than getting caught molesting a black child. Without Falwell around, the world would be a better place.

This logic is doubly stupid; it is stupid intellectually and, more important, it is stupid morally. That moralists are hypocrites isn't breaking news. Indeed, the essence of moralism is its fierce disavowal of inevitable bodily pleasures. It is impossible to be a moralist without also being a hypocrite. It didn't require carnality and a hidden camera to discredit Jerry Falwell; it required the sort of social transformation that liberals themselves stonewall. The fact that Falwell had power and a platform indicates that he said things people either believed in or wanted to hear. According to my colleague's logic, then, lots of children will need to be molested on camera for theocratic attitudes to abate. Wouldn't it be easier to empower people socially and economically so they won't gravitate to spaces where truth requires no intellectual work?

From a moral standpoint, there are too many problems to discuss, so I would merely like to ask why it is that a black child would be more scandalous than a white child or an Inuit child or a Tibetan child? To assign an ethnic status on this hypothetical child in order to amplify a rhetorical point is to buttress the worst dimensions of racism as a historical force in American society. Yes, my colleague's insinuation is that Falwell was racist in addition to latently homosexual and predatory. But Falwell was racist partly because people like my colleague allowed him to be.

Think about it: we can deconstruct my colleague's statement – a wish, really – for days and in so doing generate mounting indignation. Mostly, though, it's simply disgusting that he is willing to subject a child to abuse in order to end Jerry Falwell's career – that is, to enhance his liberal pleasure. To render the child non-white illustrates that my colleague is well aware of the value to the privileged of the most disenfranchised among us.

The shared characteristic of all these slogans and statements is that each speaker self-identifies as an advocate of justice without having any real awareness of those most in need of justice. In fact, each speaker manages to nullify those most in need of justice even as he or she pretends to speak on their behalf. And that's the problem: these liberal salvos for justice are fundamentally unjust. They are so common because they create a need for perpetual intervention.

Solutions to longstanding problems can be complex things, but the solution to this problem, in existence since 1492, is easy: morality need not be moralism, and it should never be trained on safeguarding political world-views and institutions. People will treat it better. Morality is engaging all others as moral equals. This ethic in itself will not change the world. But it's the necessary beginning to worldly change.

Sooner or later, black, Iraqi, Mexican, Indigenous, and Palestinian children will emerge from dank hotel rooms, sweat-shops, bunkers, and colonial prisons. They will link arms and compose the following letter:

> Dear Concerned Liberals: We are humans who do not want to be props in ungenerous moral formulations. We are margin-dwellers. We are the dispossessed. We are your familiar strangers. We carry silent histories on our shoulders. We have tons of behalfs that you like to speak on. We are entrapped in gruesome oxymora. We eagerly await the day when the power-less cease to be indispensably expendable.

I was called up
to commit genocide

I am the victim and perpetrator of genocide. I have been displaced by a force of cultural brutality that has obliged me to become culturally brutal. I have lent my name to those who covet human slaughter.

I am an Arab Christian.

My existence defies moral intelligibility.

I have never identified myself in an essay or tagline as a Christian because until recently being Christian simply hasn't been that important to me, at least not explicitly. Christianity is a crucial element of who am I. Because I am Arab, to be Christian is to be locked into a particular cultural space and to claim ownership over an enduring, if oblique, history. But I don't practice Christianity in a normally devout fashion. I am merely Christian. I say so as a cultural identifier and not as a profession of belief or an accrual of spiritual character.

Let me put it this way: I could not rightly be a Christian were I not also an Arab.

In my life as a writer and academic I have preferred to conceptualize myself as a participant in national communities that are simultaneously abstract and distinct. These communities are abstract because they arise from inter-communal worldviews that eschew religious background; they are distinct because they prioritize ethnic identity. I identify myself, then, as an Arab or an Arab American, the word *Arab* intimating ethnic origin and *Arab American* communal belonging. I avoid delegating myself into various religious identities that might contravene ideals of ethnic and national unity. For example, I feel a real affinity with Jordanian and Palestinian Muslims but not with most white American Christians.

But lately, for the first time in my life, I've identified an affiliation with what otherwise has been an entrenched dimension of my identity. I have come into this identification because I have been ushered into it unwittingly.

Something of a culture war has emerged around Arab Christians, Palestinians especially. One effect of this culture war is to replace the tangible humanity of Arab Christians with ethereal symbolism. This culture war also positions Arab Christians as props rather than participants in a debate of serious concern to them. Its most immediate effect, though, is to render Arab Christians complicit in the promulgation of genocide.

The promulgation of genocide is most alarming but let's nevertheless start with ethereal symbolism because Arab Christians cannot become accomplices to genocide unless they are made to exist as handmaids rather than as humans. The culture war around Arab Christians has arisen largely because of the recent interest that American evangelical dispensationalists, or Christian Zionists, have taken in them. Christian Zionists include in their ranks such influential leaders as the late Jerry Falwell, Tim LaHaye, and Pat Robertson. There is no shortage of politicians somehow in their employ and media empires have arisen from dispensationalist theology.

Recently, dispensationalists have been claiming that Palestinian Christians are a dwindling population in the Holy Land. This claim is entirely true. Palestinian Christians, who at one point constituted 15-20 percent of Palestine's Arab population, now number around 2 percent. A Palestine without Christians is abstractly foreseeable. The dispensationalists attribute this exodus to the brutality of Palestinian Muslims. This claim is completely indemonstrable and viciously false.

In this sort of discourse, Palestinian Christians become appropriated into a political stance they oppose profoundly. The political stance facilitates the very phenomenon that has engendered their dwindling numbers: Jewish colonization of Palestine. If the dispensationalists have their way, the remaining Christians in Palestine would be subjected to genocide, as would their 5 million Muslim brethren.

Christian Zionists believe unflaggingly in the right of Jews to colonize Palestine, a process they view as the restoration of biblical Israel and as the necessary precursor to rapture. According to this schema, the Palestinians, both Muslim and Christian, have few options, none of them resulting in political solvency or the ability to access human rights. Most dispensationalists call for the Palestinians to be removed forcibly to Jordan, where they can supposedly form their own state (or do anything else they please, as long as they don't disrupt the Jewish redemption of Israel). Some of those in support of this policy observe that Palestinians refusing to leave will simply have to be slaughtered. The more enlightened Christian Zionists, a demographic that is more than just oxymoronically insignificant, are open to Palestinians remaining in the Holy Land in small numbers, as long as those few Palestinians submit themselves completely to Jewish domination.

In other words, dispensationalist ideology encourages Israel to ethnically cleanse Palestinians, all Palestinians, including those who happen to be Christian. Dispensationalists have of late discovered that Palestinian Christians nevertheless can be invoked in the service of this genocide, their fate as its victim, of course, notwithstanding. This appropriation would be impossible without the transformation of Palestinian Christians from humanity into metonymy.

And the more personal reality is absolute: because Christian Zionists are evoking Palestinian Christians in order to facilitate genocide, I have become implicated at least indirectly in its rhetorical lexicon. My sympathies mean nothing to this process of implication, and my filial relationship with the subjects of this genocide is merely a curious incongruity. Those who allow themselves to be appropriated unwittingly into stances they would consciously oppose become complicit through unawareness or eventually through apathy. Like anybody else, Arab

Christians have both a right and a need to articulate their own stances.

About this business of Israeli genocide, which surely has compelled some readers to focus on semantics, I would draw a distinction between the current political situation in Israel/Palestine and the situation desired by Christian Zionists, which is of concern here. There is serious debate around what Israel has done to the Palestinians in the past and what it continues to do to them now, and all sorts of terminology can be (and has been) applied to the policies and practices of Israeli colonization. The Israeli sociologist Baruch Kimmerling, for instance, used the word *politicide*, a word affixed on political access. The Palestinian literary scholar Edward Said was fond of *dispossession*, a term broad in scope but trained on moral reproach. A passel of writers, myself included, tend toward *ethnic cleansing*, an unambiguous descriptor that nevertheless connotes differently than *genocide*.

Some folks, however, do prefer the brutally forthright word *genocide* for a variety of reasons, foremost among them the fact that Israel's stated goal long has been to maintain a Jewish demographic majority. This goal has for decades begotten policies intended to eradicate the presence of a Palestinian culture, some of them using the obvious syllogism that removing a people is the most effective way of expunging their culture.

What many dispensationalists visualize, on the other hand, would be a trenchant genocide, on a par with the worst instances of the act throughout history. They propose a forcible population transfer on an enormous scale, or outright slaughter based solely on Palestinian (i.e. non-Jewish) ethnicity, the most commonly understood form of genocide (though genocide doesn't only entail the actual murder of people). Let's keep this distinction in mind as we continue, the one delineating a more brutal alternative to extant Israeli brutality, whatever we call it.

It is because of this desired genocide that I have decided to exercise my filial right to speak as an Arab Christian. It is a way of asserting my voice in spaces it has begun, despite my reluctance, to occupy. And it is a way to shift the framework of the conversation around religion and ethnicity in the United States.

I've noticed that people like to refer to me as an 'Arab Christian' when they describe my work, though my work doesn't really describe my identity in these terms (one notable exception is a section on Christian Zionism in *Anti-Arab Racism in the USA*). A post on one blog, for example, observes, 'Steven Salaita is an Arab Christian, Professor of English, and the author of...' (If sequences illuminate priorities, then I suppose I should point out that being a professor is of more gravity to my identity than being Christian.) Other blogs and open forums also tack on 'Arab Christian' to the end of my name.

At a presentation on Christian Zionism to the Council on the National Interest, Robert O. Smith referred to me as 'an Arab Christian scholar.' The gentlemanly Smith had asked me in advance if he could refer to me as such; I responded that I would be delighted if he did, precisely because of the nature of the description, which purported in that framework to illustrate that Arab Christians don't want to be appropriated into the rapturous discourse of folks like Pat Robertson and Gary Bauer. Smith's use of the word attempted to orient Christian identity in an ethnic and historical praxis as opposed to its brassy political utility in dispensationalist usage.

Yet it's still crucial to note that to identify somebody with my politics and stated affiliations as an 'Arab Christian' is to perform a specific rhetorical act, one that hopes to convince Americans to engage Arabs as humans rather than barbarians. The word 'Christian,' despite is modification by the adjective 'Arab,' establishes an imagined reciprocation in which some type of familiarity can be generated. It is this imagined (or desired) familiarity that presumably might compel Americans to recognize humanity rather than strangeness in Arabs, the Palestinians especially. Describing me as an 'Arab Christian' thus asks those who read my work about anti-Arab racism, Israeli ethnic cleansing, and American imperialism to give that work a chance rather than dismissing it as typical Muslim disgruntlement.

The problem, though, is that it's not a good idea to employ rhetorical acts that ask others to seek familiarity as the basis of intellectual engagement; moral probity should instead be the standard. Imagined affinities have more than a whiff of groupthink inscribed in them and thus the potential for all kinds of ugly outcomes.

Or, to put it more simply, it's unfair (and arguably racist) to attribute Muslim discord about Israeli and American policies to cultural pathology or learned politics, which is exactly what people do when they decide that it's better for a Christian to break the news about Israeli brutality or American stupidity to other Christians, even if that's not what they mean to do. It's not hard to work out the imperatives underlying this conclusion. That an Arab Christian will have more legitimacy as a spokesperson in the United States against Israeli ethnic cleansing is likely true. The point is to question what we sacrifice as intellectual agents when we succumb to this reality. The most conspicuous item sacrificed is the ability of Muslims to articulate truth without Christian incredulity. Arab Muslims shouldn't have to invoke the existence of Arab Christians as an entrée into the public forum. The fact of this built-in Christian legitimacy is cause for concern and worthy of extirpation because its extirpation would foreground a necessary shift in the attitudes of Christian Americans toward Arabs and Muslims.

I can also state the matter in a slightly different way: I don't want to have to be Christian to be worth listening to in the United States. I and my Muslim brethren should be worth listening to because we have something worthwhile to say. If we cease to say things of interest then we should be ignored. Arab Muslims, however, should not be ignored simply because their religious origin fails to evoke a filiated sympathy. The rhetorical trick of identifying Christian background in Arab intellectuals runs the risk of further defamiliarizing the vast majority of voices in the Arab World.

Sooner or later, Americans are going to have to come to terms with the Arabs based on who Arabs are and not on what Americans want Arabs to be. Even though I am Christian I have little in common with non-Arab Christian Americans unless their politics are trained on real Palestinian liberation or on abolishing liberal racism in the United States. My being Christian, then, shouldn't be held up as a rhetorical handshake if I suspect that my partner's left hand hides crossed fingers behind his back. Besides, identifying my religion is redundant and only validates the sort of ignorance that I believe supplements Israel's ability to displace and colonize Palestinians. Anybody who knows anything about the Arab World will recognize that with a name like 'Steven' I am Christian; the more knowledgeable can offer an educated guess (correctly) that specifically my name signifies Orthodox Christian background.

The question of strategy isn't so easy to brush off, though. A close friend of mine, a distinctly intelligent Muslim Arab American, believes strongly that Palestinian Christians are the key to shifting Christian Americans away from their largely pro-Israel attitudes. The idea is to invoke their totemic impulses (which, like all other things that pretend to be impulsive, are socialized). This thinking is similar to some basic premisses in fields like anthropology and conflict resolution, which posit that group interests regulate social organization and that group identity seriously influences economic and political decision-making. Therefore, if Americans are made to recognize an intrinsic affiliation with Palestinians and not with Israelis, then the tenets of group identity will dictate a shift in political outlook. This type of strategy is essentially realistic and is trained less on moral or philosophical contingencies than on quantifiable results.

I admire this strategy but ultimately find it problematic. I don't like to state my reaction from within a pro–con paradigm because I'd like for it to be more complex than mere agreement or disagreement. (There are numerous ways to achieve political goals and to produce a moral analysis, but neither goals nor analyses are achieved without multitudes, sometimes harmonious and other times discordant.) Likewise, I wouldn't argue that this strategy is a poor one or even that it wouldn't be effective. It is highly likely to be effective, at least in local spaces. I'm merely curious as to the costs of its effectiveness and what is sacrificed in the short term of the strategy's implementation and how those sacrifices affect the long-term outlook of both Palestinians and Arab Americans.

The Palestinian population in the Occupied Territories, for example, is 97 percent Muslim and approximately 2 percent Christian (there are smaller Palestinian religious minorities, such as the Druze and Bahai). The 2 percent of Christians can suitably represent the 97 percent of Muslims insofar as Palestinian Muslims and Christians share a common history, culture, and political vision. Yet it is precisely because of these shared phenomena that a privileging of the Christian minority on behalf of the entire society is dubious. Introducing Palestinian liberatory politics through Christian spokespeople makes the politics sound more legitimate to Americans. There's no doubt that those politics, which are not only legitimate but also morally requisite, need to be taken more seriously by Americans. The problem is that raising those politics by privileging Palestinian Christians doesn't itself legitimize or delegitimize the politics. It amplifies them without altering them. In other words, introducing Palestinian liberatory politics through Christian spokespeople only makes those politics *sound* more legitimate, but it doesn't actually legitimize them. It creates a perception of legitimacy that lasts only as long as Islam remains suppressed. Americans need finally to come to grips with a human version of Islam that allows them to take Muslims and their grievances seriously. Short of this transformation, Arab Christians are nothing more than a mesmeric chimera.

This is one of the reasons why I consider myself a participant in ethnic and national, not religious, identities. I want Palestinian Christians to be liberated and I want them to live in a functional democracy that protects human rights, but I want this for them in addition to Palestinian Muslims. I am therefore bound morally to inclusive approaches that advance multiconfessional national goals.

Anyway, ethnic minorities in the United States and colonized populations around the world have a shared interest in subverting the tacit equation of mainstream American politics with normative integrity through the demand that others conform to mainstream American standards of normativity. Featuring Arab Christians as the face of Palestine in order to generate familiar feelings among Americans subtly reinforces this pervasive standard of normativity.

Yet this moment demands the articulation of Arab Christian voices in the United States because of the dispensationalist claim that Christians are being driven from the Holy Land through the perfidy of Palestinian Muslims.

On an elemental level, I want to assert an Arab Christian identity simply to invoke the authority to state: I am an Arab Christian. Do not use me to support genocide. You have no right to invoke my name, my culture, my history, and my ancestors to embolden our colonizers. We did not ask for your intervention on our behalf; we reject your peculiar altruism. We stand in solidarity with our Palestinian Muslim brothers and sisters, our fellow victims of ethnic cleansing by the Jews to whom you have provided unremitting philosophical and financial support. We reject your false claims and refuse to be deployed in the service of our own destruction.

Palestinian Christians have responded more or less thusly. In 2006, for instance, the heads of all the churches in Jerusalem released a widely disseminated and strongly worded statement that began, 'We categorically reject Christian Zionist doctrines as false teaching that corrupts the biblical message of love, justice, and reconciliation.' The statement also affirmed that 'Palestinians are one people, both Muslim and Christian. We reject all attempts to subvert and fragment their unity.' Other Arab Christians have gone public with professions of solidarity with fellow Arabs, as when a delegation of Arab Americans including Deborah Najor, Nadine Naber, and Warren David held a press conference in Detroit in the summer of 2006 to condemn Israel specifically as Arab Christians.

There are other reasons to talk back to dispensationalists as Arab Christians. By expressing concern, however phony, for the Christians of Palestine, dispensationalists imply at least an oblique affinity between themselves and Palestinian Christians.

In reality, the two communities have little in common. The religiously inclined among Palestine's Christians believe Jesus Christ to be the son of God and believe in the veracity of the biblical crucifixion, just as do all dispensationalists. This is their primary, and only, similarity. I would doubt that folks like Tom DeLay and Hal Lindsey care, but Arab Christians generally detest Christian Zionists (I imagine the reasons are by now obvious). Arab Christians also feel no historical or cultural affinity with the dispensationalists, who adhere to a markedly different theology and interpretation of scripture. The vast majority of Christians in Palestine are invested deeply in the ethos of belonging to the world's only community of indigenous Christians and being an axial component of an oppressed Palestinian nation. Unless Christian Zionists abandon their support of Israel, they will never have the ability to speak on behalf of Palestinian Christians except as they do at present, as liars and interlopers.

Another obvious reason that Arab Christians might assert their filiated identities vis-à-vis dispensationalists is for the sake of basic truth, although one needn't belong to any particular ethnic group or nationality to raise the basic truth that Christian Zionists are completely wrong about the reasons for Christian emigration from Palestine. First of all, we need to be clear that tens of thousands of Palestinian Christians have been displaced at various points since 1948, and to classify this displacement as emigration would be a gross bastardization of history. The historian Sami Hadawi has illustrated, to provide only one example, that in 1948 over half of West Jerusalem's

Christians were expelled by Jews from their homes, the largest ever numerical decline of Palestinian Christians. The Melkite priest Elias Chacour has written passionately about the displacement of the entire Christian population of the Galilean village of Biram and its subsequent destruction by the Israeli army. Palestinian Christians have story after hideous story of displacement and the consequent miseries of life under the Israeli occupation.

Next, it is worth pointing out that nowadays Palestinian Muslims are emigrating in greater numbers than Palestinian Christians (even adjusted for numerical disparities). The notion that Palestinian Christians are escaping Muslim perfidy, then, confronts an inconvenient reality that exposes its racist causality. The only judicious response to that inconvenient reality is to ponder why the Muslims are emigrating (assuming, of course, that we will dispense with the thesis that Muslims are emigrating because of Muslims). The answers are wide-ranging and have to do with economic possibilities, family ties abroad, political instability, an absence of civil liberties, and governmental corruption. Palestinian emigration also has much to do with the Israeli occupation, which amplifies the more universal reasons that human populations migrate and emigrate.

The reasons for this Palestinian emigration are remarkably complex, which in itself undermines the simplistic explanation of Muslim brutality. In any case, the Palestinians, who have a profound attachment to their ancestral land, haven't been emigrating in particularly large numbers; they do so at around the same rate as Israeli Jews, who, as the ethnic group with all of the Holy Land's social and economic power, cannot rightly blame it on Muslim oppression. Anyway, the premiss that Palestinian Muslims oppress Palestinian Christians is incorrect. The two groups, which together comprise the same national community, have a history of coexistence that is rare in spaces encompassing a clear religious minority. This is so partly because of the influence of Christian pathos on the Holy Land, but also because Palestinian Christians have played a strong role in the formation of Palestinian nationalist politics and have long been an intellectual and economic power in Palestinian society. (See, for better or worse, the role of figures such as George Habash, Naif Al-Mutawa, Atallah Henna, Hanan Ashrawi, Azmi Beshara, Emile Habiby, Suha Arafat, George Antonius, and Huwaida Arraf.) More than anything, though, Palestinian Muslims can boast a grand history of open-mindedness.

We are left to wonder how, given their integral role in Palestinian culture and politics, it is that Palestinian Christians are oppressed by their Muslim compatriots. Christian Zionists claim that it is because of the preponderance of intolerance among Muslims based on the rise of Islamist politics. This claim is worth engaging because it is superficially true and underlies a variety of relevant contemporary Middle Eastern politics.

There certainly is wariness among Arab Christians, in Palestine and elsewhere, about the rise of Islamist politics. As a religious minority, Arab Christians are right to worry about what might happen to them in the event of a theocratic coup (as does anybody who values the sort of liberty that never has existed in theocratic governments of all faiths). However, it would be disingenuous to limit this anxiety to the Arab World's Christian population, as many Muslims are likewise wary of religious politics. More important, there is no evidence to suggest that Arab Christian wariness of Islamism stimulates emigration decisively or even indirectly. Few Arab Christians cite Islamist politics as their primary reason for emigrating to Europe or the United States; they overwhelmingly attribute it, as do all Asian émigrés, to economic opportunity. Islamism contributes to a general political instability in the Arab World that in turn instigates economic problems, but it by no means exclusively sets these forces in motion. Other factors, such as aggressive American foreign policy, Western material support for Arab tyrants, and the encroachment of Israel onto Arab territory, are equally or more important.

Finally, it's crucial to make clear that while dispensational-ists imply that the emigration of Christians from Palestine threatens the existence of a unique culture, in fact Palestinian Christian culture is quite alive in places such as Chile, the United States, Honduras, Canada, Great Britain, and else-where. Palestinian Christian culture also will always be alive in Palestine, because as long as Israel doesn't completely bar Christians from entering their holy sites then a cultural pres-ence will continue to circulate throughout the land. There is no Palestine without a Christian presence. That presence is integral to the landscape and to the indigenous culture belonging to that landscape. Israel has set out to destroy both the landscape and its indigenous culture, and so it presents the only realistic threat of destruction of a Christian presence in the Holy Land. Israel will have accomplished the destruction of this Christian presence only through the elimination of all Palestinians. Even if they desired to (they don't), Palestinian Muslims cannot destroy the Christian presence because it is a part of who they are culturally and historically. This is a basic fact that Christian Zionists either refuse to understand or choose to approach with barefaced ignorance.

And this is the main point of it all in my estimation: if I take a moment to assert a filiated identity and speak as an Arab Christian it is primarily because there are truths to our existence in this world and nuances in our varied participation in cultural and national communities. The Christian Zionists haven't accessed or articulated any of those truths. They aren't intellectually disposed to nuance. It is up to us, then, to do it – not on their behalf, but for our own well-being as indigenous Christians.

I am deeply uncomfortable being invoked by scoundrels and theocrats to justify colonization and dispossession.

I am not bemused by the morbid irony of Christian Zionists, who have forced Palestinian Christians to celebrate their own displacement and destruction.

They called me up to commit genocide. I participated in that genocide the entire time I was silent.

Then I asserted a birthright that was stolen from me and spoke as an Arab Christian.

But I am aware that there comes a point when voices need to revert back to more familiar vocalizations.

So I would like to drop again my filiated identity as an Arab Christian and speak through a more basic filiation as a human being: the Christian Zionist desire to induce genocide of Palestinian Muslims is worthy of vocal condemnation, but also requires an intellectual intervention that takes seriously cultural and political multiformity in the Arab World. In this sense, the entire conversation around Islam and Arabs in the United States should evolve toward moral variance rather than reproducing truisms about premodern and primordial culture.

I should confess to a personal stake in this argument: it is only through this moral variance that I, an individual assembled through communal identities, can become morally intelligible. I wouldn't have access to a Christian identity, after all, without the ubiquity of being Arab.

Open-mindedness
on Independence Day

O f course, not all African Americans are lazy. Of course, not all Indians are alcoholics. Of course, not all Jews are stingy. Of course, not all Russians are whores. Of course, not all Mexicans are dirty. Of course, not all Pakistanis smell. Of course, not all Africans are bestial. Of course, not all Eskimos use 250 words for snow.

Of course, not all Asians are craven. Of course, not all Americans are ignorant. Of course, not all Japanese are kamikazes. Of course, not all Indians are stoic. Of course, not all African Americans are criminal. Of course, not all Arabs are angry. Of course, not all Maoris are premodern. Of course, not all Hawaiians are hula dancers. Of course, not all Aborigines are backward. Of course, not all Thai are gamblers. Of course, not all women are too emotional.

Of course, not all Mexicans are laborers. Of course, not all South Asians are swindlers. Of course, not all Appalachians are backwoods rapists. Of course, not all poor folk are tasteless. Of course, not all women are mentally inferior. Of course, not all Poles are stupid. Of course, not all Italians are Mafiosi. Of course, not all Spaniards are sleazy. Of course, not all Afghans are filthy. Of course, not all Hispanics are greasy. Of course, not all homosexuals are child molesters. Of course, not all Africans are nude and pagan. Of course, not all Sri Lankans deserve it.

'Of course, not all Muslims are terrorists.' (Thomas Friedman, *New York Times*, July 4, 2007)

Michael Moore does it again

When discussing somebody like Michael Moore, an artist fixated on selling rather than testing political hypotheses, it's probably best to avoid the appearance of cunning or obliqueness. Let me then go ahead at the outset and define 'it': the act of professing liberal political viewpoints through the partial use of illicit racism as an unacknowledged rhetorical device. Michael Moore excels at 'it.' His last two documentary films, *Fahrenheit 911* and *Sicko*, employ the device to largely unsuspected perfection. Moore certainly didn't invent that device, but he exemplifies its utility to the documentary film genre and its indispensability to American liberal politics more broadly. The two films disavow inequality and advocate justice through the corresponding but unexamined presence of anti-Arab racism.

I want to focus here primarily on *Sicko*, partly because I've already commented publicly on *Fahrenheit 911* and partly because I find in it a more understated and thus analytically useful example of how a subtle, almost invisible, anti-Arab racism underlies one of Moore's rhetorical strategies.

My dislike of *Fahrenheit 911* foregrounds my negative reaction to *Sicko*. It's easy to dislike *Fahrenheit 911*, though. The film not only uses illicit racism as an unacknowledged rhetorical device, it sometimes relies on explicitly racist imagery. I'm thinking of the Orientalist scenery Moore employs when he mentions Morocco, which includes monkeys and – what else? – a tarbush (fez). I have already written about my objection to the manner in which Moore explores the USA Patriot Act. In brief, I found it bothersome that Moore chose a group of elderly white people who were mildly inconvenienced by the FBI as exemplars of the Patriot Act's dangers. I saw this move as a tacit endorsement of anti-Arab racism because in ignoring the Patriot Act's primary victims, Arabs and Muslims, Moore chose a deceitful approach he believed would be convincing to mainstream Americans. That approach can be effective, however, based solely on the assumption that white activists necessarily are innocent of wrongdoing while Arabs and Muslims are unavoidably suspicious. In other words, truth didn't matter to Moore; getting his point across was more important to him.

Thus the modus operandi of Michael Moore: he ignores anything that might undermine or complicate his staunchly liberal commitments.

This objection mentions nothing of the most insidious form of anti-Arab racism in *Fahrenheit 911*, a film that portrays Arabs as shady oil barons and menacing sheikhs. In the film, a bumbling, malicious George Bush, Jr., is shown to be in the toils of his Arab benefactors, who provide a shadowy foil to the fundamental American goodness Moore urges his audience to restore. Other than greedy, robe-swathed oil barons, Arabs in *Fahrenheit 911* are monumentally romanticized Iraqis who, according to Moore, lived peacefully in Saddam Hussein's Iraq before Dubya came along and ruined everything. Either way, Arabs don't actually have a voice in *Fahrenheit 911*. They exist as overwrought spectacles in Moore's dogmatic vision.

Moore has never been much of an advocate of nuance. His work selectively utilizes evidence so that Moore can convey a predetermined thesis. When my undergraduate students employ Moore's specialty, bending evidence to fit an argument rather than the other way around, I grade them down. Moore is a talented filmmaker with a likeable personality; however, as a rhetorician he is at an early undergraduate level. At least inexperienced undergraduates have a passable excuse. With Moore, we are forced to conclude dishonesty if we do not accept inability as a valid reason. Indeed, should his film career sputter, I'm sure that the tourism departments of Canada, France, Great Britain, and Cuba would love to hire Moore. He romanticizes each of these nations as the glorious opposite of a particular American failure (mainly gun control and healthcare). In *Bowling for Columbine*, for example, Moore totes his camera to Ontario to illustrate that racism is a distinctly American problem, more or less absent in Canada. In *Sicko*, he asks us to believe that the British healthcare system engenders well-to-do physicians and problem-free medical attention. Moore trades in the art of persuasion and not in the artistry of truthfulness. He turns up precisely the result he set out to discover.

Even if one agrees with some or all of Moore's arguments – and there is much about them to admire – I find it difficult to accept the manner in which he presents them, which is duplicitous and insulting. Moore is a perfect example of why artists and intellectuals should pursue unaffiliated exposition. To service a certain political affiliation is to forgo the possibility that the affiliated party is worthy of the scrutiny we will direct at its opposition. To affiliate ourselves forces us into an arbitrated intellectual space. In producing a documentary in the service of John Kerry's 2004 presidential campaign, for instance, Moore ignored Democratic collusion in the very things about which he waxed indignant.

The point isn't to debate whether Moore is correct that healthcare in the United States is inequitable and a national disgrace. Of course it's a disgrace, and only an insurance lobbyist or an idiot would argue that the current system of HMOs and corporate medicine is equitable. The point is that in making a documentary about this current system Moore accidentally highlights other national problems, their mere existence in his film a glaring reminder of his own artistic and political complicity.

I wish Moore would be more analytically rigorous than he chooses to be. *Sicko* resorts to gimmicks to make what otherwise is a straightforward and crucial point about the dreadful state of healthcare in America. The evidence Moore amasses against stingy insurance companies is both germane and powerful. The film's irascible tone, a Moore staple, is more knowing than righteous. And Moore, as he has noted repeatedly in interviews, is working with material that is fundamentally bipartisan and that can traverse party interests among Americans. Everybody wants adequate healthcare for themselves and their families. Apropos of this basic wish (and human right), few people who aren't paid by insurance companies for their sympathies are apt to sympathize with detached and seemingly omnipotent HMOs.

Moore didn't need to rely on gimmicks, which render *Sicko* a purveyor of unjust values. Their inclusion exemplifies Moore's entrapment in a type of liberalist discourse that will never enable him to perform the sort of revolutionary interventions that ostensibly inspire his work. (In case anybody fancies me too overblown, this liberalist discourse will never enable Moore to perform even pacific interventions.) In a broader sense, their inclusion in *Sicko* intimates Moore's acceptance of anti-Arab racism as an effective motivating force in the United States. The unjust values Moore reproduces and the unjust values he attacks are related, despite being far from identical, because they arise from the same impulse among their advocates to ultimately appease centers of power.

The most conspicuous gimmick in *Sicko*, the one I have in mind here, is the scene in which Moore apparently sails from Miami to Guantánamo Bay in Cuba. With Moore are white – nearly all victims of the healthcare industry in *Sicko* are white – 9/11 rescue workers with recurrent health problems. The workers have been unable to obtain adequate medical coverage. Moore, having heard Republican Senator (and physician) Bill

Frist boasting on television that the prisoners on the US military base at Guantánamo receive excellent healthcare, decides to see if that healthcare will be available to the 9/11 workers. The curiosity, of course, is tongue-in-cheek. Moore knows that the 9/11 workers won't receive any treatment at Guantánamo, and so by taking them there he orchestrates a scene replete with ironic commentary. The ironic commentary might have achieved the status of droll or illuminating if he didn't have to rely on the customary tactic of dehumanizing Muslims in order to applaud patriotic Americans. I would instead assign the scene the status of tacitly racist.

There are many reasons for this judgment. Before I get to them, though, let's unpack the meanings of the Guantánamo scene. Moore manages to say many important things simultaneously, a difficult thing to do. It is not with the complexity of the scene that I take issue; I take issue with one of the scene's tacit commentaries. On its face, the scene is a way to drive home the point that the American healthcare system is unjust, given that it excludes even those who have nobly served the United States. Less explicitly, it re-creates a sort of Kafkaesque absurdity that Moore highlights elsewhere: American heroes need to visit a secretive military prison surrounded by enemy territory in order to access what should be their birthright as citizens of a wealthy, technologically advanced nation.

The scene also provides an ironic commentary, because Moore doesn't give viewers the impression that he actually believes Frist's claim about excellent healthcare in Guantánamo. He is taking the prison to task by exposing its own healthcare discourse as a myth. Moore thus condemns two hypocrisies, one related to corporate healthcare and the other to torture at Guantánamo. (Moore is on record opposing the existence of the prison.) Neither the 9/11 workers nor the prisoners at Guantánamo are being treated fairly. Only the 9/11 workers, however, are presented as worthy of sympathy.

One might object to my argument by noting that *Sicko* is a film about the American healthcare system, not the military prison at Guantánamo. I would reply to this objection by agreeing wholeheartedly, and would add merely that Moore should have then stuck to the subject. The moment he involved Guantánamo and the people suffering in its prison he became morally accountable for that material. By not exercising such accountability, Moore ended up exploiting Guantánamo's prisoners. I do not use the verb 'exploit' lightly, and don't mean to imply that Moore's exploitation is on a par with the American government's vis-à-vis the prison. Unlike pregnancy or coincidences, exploitation has gray areas, and Moore's is not pernicious. It is nevertheless problematic.

Here is how Moore explained the scene on *Democracy Now!*

And I thought, well, you know, here we have the 9/11 rescue workers who can't get any healthcare. Here they are trumpeting how they have free universal healthcare, dental care, eye care, nutrition counseling, for the detainees. And I thought, well, why don't we just take our 9/11 workers down to Gitmo and see if we can get some of that free healthcare they're bragging about? And so, essentially, when you see the film – I don't want to give the whole thing away – but that's essentially what we go to do.

This reasoning is clever on its face, but lamentable morally. We could, for example, extend Moore's logic: why don't we see if we can experience some of that torture they're concealing?

More damningly, Moore invokes a set of serious issues that he immediately elides. The detainees, referred to variously as 'terror suspects,' 'suspected terrorists,' 'enemy combatants,' and 'al-Qaeda,' are rendered props in Moore's rhetorical circus and are thus precluded from the luxury of basic human identification. They are exploited, then, because Moore appropriates them for a specific purpose that has nothing to do with their own well-being. Here the Guantánamo prisoners become dehumanized tableaux. We can't take them seriously. In fact, we're not compelled to care one whit about them. But they're saddled with the burden of generating sympathy for Americans.

Sicko assumes that the prisoners in Guantánamo are guilty by refusing to comment on the dubious rationales for many of the detainees' captivity, among whose ranks are children and people long found innocent by American courts and investigators. In the most generous interpretation, Moore merely omits why the prison and the prisoners are there in the first place, and he evades even perfunctory mention of why Guantánamo is so deplorable. He indeed presents an irony abstractly favorable to the prisoners, but this irony – the prisoners not actually receiving healthcare, but torture – is too soft to be effective. Moore only explores the irony long enough to make his point about suffering white American heroes. Beyond these white heroes, he doesn't at all contextualize Guantánamo.

This sort of move is in keeping with the tenor of Moore's

oeuvre. Moore panders to what he imagines to be the furtive prejudices of his audience. Liberal white America and centrist Democrats won't identify with black people? No problem. Moore will only include them peripherally. Oppositional but ultimately patriotic Americans will refuse to accept the humanity of Arabs and Muslims? Fine. Moore will transform the objects of their opposition, such as the Patriot Act, into a white issue, tossing in images of villainous Arabs to provide comfort. Guantánamo is a useful contrivance but too heavy a topic for multiplexes, Harvey Weinstein, and *Good Morning America*? Why, the solution is practically foreordained. Moore will appropriate Guantánamo into a liberalist paradigm that evades compassion for its Muslim captives and fancies itself a clever paean to the prison's enablers. This final move isn't merely bad filmmaking by virtue of its useless gimmickry. It is also rhetorically immoral by virtue of its unwillingness to render moral outrage comprehensive.

The scene is reminiscent of an approach Moore employs in *Fahrenheit 911*. Because that documentary was conjoined with an activist mission to elect John Kerry, Moore wanted it to reach as wide an audience as possible. Obviously, this desire entailed discursive boundaries, as did the decision to endorse the Democratic Party. (It prevented Moore from justifiably criticizing Democrats, for example.) Moore not only faithfully adhered to those boundaries, he actually shrunk them. In his zeal to produce a film that would matter, Moore found refuge in that infamous place of scoundrels. *Fahrenheit 911* is nothing more than a crude patriotic gesture disguised as art, determined to mobilize its audience in the service of corporate

politics, themselves disguised (meagerly) as radical or oppositional. Moore repeats his reliance on patriotism in *Sicko* by so
prominently featuring 9/11 rescue workers and taking them to
Guantánamo where they are juxtaposed with their antipodal
Others, Muslim terrorists.

The point of this scene is to emphasize the shamefulness of
corporate healthcare in the United States. This point should be
easy to accomplish, as Moore himself illustrates elsewhere in
Sicko. He nevertheless chose to overemphasize his point and in
so doing he created a faulty binary and proffered an attenuated
framework of selective empathy: *if it is shameful that 9/11 rescue
workers are denied healthcare, then consider just how shameful
it is that suspected Muslim terrorists are not.* Anyway, invoking
patriotism in order to persuade is a cheap and unimaginative
rhetorical device. Moore even manages to infuse his argument
with the same language and ideas from his enemies on the right:
'If al-Qaeda can get healthcare, then why can't 9/11 heroes?'
Moore reproduces the prototypical neoconservative binary
whose ideology he has spent the past seven years condemning.

More important, there is absolutely no basis other than
racist totalization on which Guantánamo's prisoners can be
referred to homogenously as 'al-Qaeda.' The prison is one of
many embarrassments associated with the Bush administration,
and has been a source of protest and outrage in British politics
since its discovery. It emblematizes the post-9/11 mainstreaming of torture in the United States. It is not, in short, a joke. It
needn't play a role in the American healthcare debate. It needs
instead to play a role in an almost non-existent conversation

in the United States about the immorality of torture and the racism of much recent legislation.

If Moore felt compelled to invoke the captives in Guantánamo, then he should have taken a moment to impart the basic (and what one wishes were intuitive) proposition that those captives are human. They are not props; they are people who have suffered tremendously, people wrested from their families and held without legal counsel in an indeterminate state. Many of them surely are guilty of something according to somebody. But many, according to extensive evidence, are guilty of nothing other than being dark-skinned and using an Arabic word to refer to God. Some are children, who are by legal definition innocent. Like the 9/11 rescue workers Moore lionizes, these humans have suffered an injustice. All of them, American, Muslim, or both, deserve our ear and our empathy if we are inclined to care about these things. Moore asks us to care about these things, but he coerces us to care incompletely.

Ultimately, *Sicko* presents us with questions about the uses and utility of art, not merely the art of exposition or persuasion but the morality of art that simultaneously endeavors to do political work. Art has been a common expository topic since the advent of writing and has inspired a range of divergent opinion spanning Aristotle to Jean Baudrillard; it has also been a topic of diverse conversation for millennia in oral-based communities. Fitting Moore into something so complex, then, may be difficult, especially since his oeuvre rather fits the paradigm not of artfulness but of rabble-rousing. I hesitate to preclude Moore from the realm of art, however, because he does his rabble-rousing through an artistic medium, film, and so he warrants evaluation through this framework like any other documentary filmmaker.

I would venture as a foundational argument the proposition that art certainly has rules but no set of rules. The rules of art shift and evolve according to the project. Art can thus be polemical or purely abstract. It always comments, though, and in that sense it is always political. Nor is art necessarily a product of truthfulness or even of purported truthfulness. It can be guileful or manipulative; sometimes it is contemptible. I adhere to no romantic belief that art needs to be beautiful or noble, or even that it needs to be meaningful. Some art is profoundly beautiful (*The God of Small Things*, *Rabbit Proof Fence*), some noble (*Common Sense*, *In the Light of Reverence*), and some meaningful (*Once Were Warriors*, *Power*). Other art possesses none of these three qualities (most of Gertrude Stein's work, for example, or some of Sherman Alexie's more irreverent short stories). I wouldn't hierarchize these examples based on any assumed criteria that say the beautiful, noble, or meaningful art is better. This sort of hierarchy would be purely conjectural and therefore fallacious. The more useful point is that art comes in all varieties regardless of how we choose to judge its quality. (I, for instance, tend to dislike art with any hint of didacticism and therefore judge it as being of lesser quality than work that is politically subtle, but I don't use this reaction as evidence that didactic work isn't art.)

But art – no matter what else it is, and ultimately it is everything – can't be one thing in particular: inflexibly affiliated.

This criterion, more than any other, separates art from propaganda. Moore's art is inflexibly affiliated to one of two things (and sometimes to both concurrently): his prearranged agenda and the Democratic Party. Democrats have mastered the art of conciliation but otherwise are as artless as truck-stop bathrooms (which, incidentally, tend to emit a more tolerable aroma). And Moore's agenda isn't a problem per se, though it usually is problematic as a political proposition. The fact that his agenda always is prearranged is bothersome. The work subsequently plays out like a fine-tuned broadcast of selective exposition. Take, for example, Moore's hypothesis that healthcare in the United States is dreadful. This is a sound hypothesis and he does a reasonable job in illuminating it and rendering it convincing. Yet Moore had decided already what the outcome of his findings would be, and so his hypothesis is convincing more by accident than through honest inquiry. Moore manipulates his hypothesis by romanticizing in the crudest way possible the healthcare systems in Great Britain, Canada, and France, which all have socialized medicine. Rather than usefully limiting the force of his claim by acknowledging some problems with those systems and thus rendering his argument nuanced, Moore makes them out to be a panacea.

This sort of move bespeaks intellectual dishonesty. It also insults viewers because Moore doesn't allow them to weigh evidence thoughtfully, or trust them to ascertain intelligent conclusions amid complex issues; he doesn't even provide them with those options. He decides what they ought to believe and then goes about constructing a narrative, any narrative, to support that decision. In this way, *Sicko* works inversely as political theater: rather than illuminating through a distinct pacing the terms of a particular discovery, Moore tempers hyperbole with personal profiles intended to coerce sympathy. These profiles, which usually feature people who have dealt with unmistakable injustice, tend to do little more than satisfy the patronizing affections of liberal benevolence.

Michael Moore is a skilled provocateur; he is a poor artist.

At one point in *Sicko*, in the build-up to the Guantánamo stunt, a female soldier complains of the detainees: 'They get way better healthcare than I do.' The inclusion of this complaint in the film exemplifies Moore's artistic shortcomings and his moral failure around the issue of racism. It exemplifies artistic shortcoming because it is a throwaway statement, a puerile un-truth that means nothing in particular but conveys an implicit hatefulness; yet Moore features the soldier's sentiment centrally in *Sicko*'s narrative, as if there is a redeemable truth inscribed in its morbid illogic. It exemplifies moral failure around the issue of racism because the simple eight-word sentence manages to dismiss one of the crucial issues of our time in the United States: torture. First of all, it is imperative we recognize that whether or not the prisoners in Guantánamo are receiving healthcare is immaterial in light of the fact that they are being tortured. The soldier in Moore's film would never trade her healthcare situation for theirs. Because she would not – and Moore knows she would not, because neither she nor he is that obtuse – her comment has no business being in the film. It is patently dishon-est, and I don't see how it is possible that Moore is unaware of its patent dishonesty. By including it, and thereby tacitly endorsing it, Moore takes ownership of that dishonesty.

More important, the soldier's complaint positions Muslims yet again as contradistinctive to a patriotic American identity. The 'I' – metonymical of the dedicated American – achieves total normativity when juxtaposed with an Islamic 'they.' Hence the most problematic dimension of Moore's filmmaking. He doesn't seem interested in offering a nuanced argument. He appears to prefer subsuming Others into subordinate relationships for rhetorical effect. In this case, such a move entailed the horridly immoral consequence of brushing away torture in the service of propaganda on behalf of the quintessential American patriot.

Moore has done it before. When I first wrote about *Fahrenheit 911* I was eager to give Moore the benefit of the doubt: I wasn't prepared to argue that the anti-Arab racism in that documentary is systematic. I conceptualized it instead as something of an unwitting by-product of poor rhetorical technique. After viewing *Sicko*, however, it is clear that Moore habitually exploits whatever Other is available to silently fortify his narrow liberalist agenda. At this moment the safest Other happens to be Arabs and Muslims – safe in the sense that they can easily be made expendable with little risk of outcry or even recognition.

Had Moore, after all, made a movie about prisoners in Guantánamo rather than a movie exploiting prisoners in Guantánamo, he would merely be another honest documentary filmmaker. And that's far less exciting than being Michael Moore, liberal hero.

Ambition, terrorism, and empathy

There's something slightly idiosyncratic about Virginia Tech, a sprawling research university in a vividly rural locale. The university's maroon and orange clash. Its most recognizable place-names – the war memorial and the drillfield – intimate a military presence that is largely past. And the university's nomenclature doesn't accurately reflect its own breadth of coverage, insinuating as it does the non-existence of comprehensive liberal arts programs.

Yet there's something highly stable and starkly logical about Virginia Tech's idiosyncrasy. The majority of students who graduate from Virginia Tech remain loyal to the university as alumni, sports fans, weekend trippers, and informal ambassadors. A specific culture exists around Virginia Tech in which students and alumni participate; describing that culture absent of direct participation would be nearly impossible. Virginia

Tech, for reasons that aren't necessarily tangible, inspires consistent and certain devotion.

I am not a Virginia Tech alumnus. I obtained two degrees from nearby Radford University, a regional comprehensive whose bread and butter were nursing and education; Radford used to be an all-women's school and a branch of the formerly all-male Virginia Tech (in those days known by the acronym VPI, from its official name: Virginia Polytechnic Institute and State University). I earned my B.S. in Political Science and my M.A. in English from Radford. As a student, I found Radford's English Department to be fantastic; I found its Political Science Department unimaginative and intellectually conservative (with the exception of one professor, Reginald Shareef). I am thankful for my education there but deem my experience unremarkable.

Truthfully, I attended Radford because I couldn't get into Virginia Tech. As a 17-year-old in nearby Bluefield, Virginia, I wasn't impressive as either a student or a young man. My grades ranged from average to embarrassing and I boasted middling SAT scores. I wasn't ready to be serious. I didn't know what I could possibly be serious about. But I found a voice and a set of interests at Radford, aided by the encouragement of some inspiring professors, and so I will be forever grateful for my college education. I sometimes felt slight envy toward those who attended Tech, in whose shadow we dwelled at the smaller and even more rural Radford.

After I completed my M.A., I entered into a doctoral program in English at the University of Oklahoma, a school that in its own way inspires permanent loyalty. (I remain quite attached to OU as an alumnus, and am openly proud to have gone there.) In Appalachia, and in Virginia particularly, Tech is something of a behemoth, a ubiquitous presence as a logo on T-shirts and bumper stickers, and a desirable place to seek learning. Outside of Appalachia, in northern Virginia, Tech alumni seem to be everywhere, and so is the presence of discordant maroon and orange. I learned, though, that beyond Virginia and Appalachia, Tech wasn't so fluently recognized. The university is nationally known and is attended by thousands of international students, but in many ways it is a regional institution.

After I completed my doctorate at OU, I started my first tenure-track position at the University of Wisconsin–Whitewater, about fifty miles southeast of Madison, a regional comprehensive similar in demographics and mission to Radford. I was happy to begin my career as an academic by serving students at an institution comparable to the one at which I was educated as an undergraduate. I never quite took to Wisconsin, though, an exilic feeling attributable to things other than bad weather. Madison is a place that in numerous ways fails to fulfill the principles of its self-image. But at heart I am an Appalachian boy. I wanted to return home.

I remember sitting in the living room of our bungalow on a summer evening in Madison with my wife, Diana. The air was redolent with Midwest balm, thick with humidity and punctured by moths bumping against the screen door and the low-timbre buzz of mosquitoes. Diana, wearing a white tank top and camouflage cargo shorts, was sprawled on the couch, sipping iced tea. Shirtless, I tinkered with a gold crucifix resting in a nest of chest hair as I fidgeted in my recliner to avoid sticking to the fabric. The sonance of heavy air surrounded us. 'I want to go back on the job market,' I informed her, out of nowhere.

Over excessive cigarettes, we had a long conversation that night about where we wanted our life to go. Leaving Wisconsin wasn't really of concern; where we might end up dominated our discussion. As always, Diana was flexible and open-minded. If I felt that it was time to seek a different job, she would support me.

'Where would you most like to be offered a professorship?' she asked after we had decided that I would re-enter the job market, a time-consuming undertaking, in the fall.

I had already published my first book and had two under contract at scholarly presses. I therefore felt that I could be competitive at the assistant professor level. I contemplated the usual suspects: Stanford, Harvard, Cornell, Northwestern. With my state-school degrees, though, I knew that it would take more than publications to attract such universities. Anyway, we both agreed that we'd prefer to be near our parents in Virginia, so I pondered a regional list of the post-secondary elite: Duke, Georgetown, UVa, Johns Hopkins.

'Virginia Tech,' I finally responded. I didn't think about Virginia Tech until that moment. The answer seemed to come from outside of me, but once it arrived I couldn't shake it. 'Yeah,' I continued, wrapping my mind around the idea, 'wouldn't it be crazy if I got a job at Virginia Tech?'

'Yeah, it would.' I could see Diana trying to wrap her mind around the possibility, steadily warming to the idea.

When the job ads were released a few months later, in September, I was relieved to find that a number of solid research universities were hiring in my areas of interest. Those who have experienced a humanities job search know that position descriptions are unreliable. They contain myriad subtexts and hidden meanings. Only the search committees that put them together have a decent sense of who might best fit their wishes (and this isn't always the case). Job candidates who encounter their dream jobs on paper, then, often are baffled and disappointed when they don't even procure screening interviews. I was aware of this reality. Nevertheless, I couldn't help but perk up when I saw that Virginia Tech was seeking an assistant professor of American literature. The job description seemed to be tailored specifically to my scholarly interests and publication record. It was my dream job. I decided then that I would be the person Virginia Tech hired.

Diana and I wanted our life to go to Blacksburg.

After an extensive interview process, I was offered and subsequently accepted a professorship in the English Department. I had bonded with members of the search committee and felt comfortable on campus during my two-day visit in January. I had received other job offers, one of which I considered seriously, but ultimately Diana and I decided to make the move back to Appalachia.

A few months into the job, which I ended up enjoying even more than I had anticipated, I was at a barbeque in North

Carolina where a family friend couldn't believe that I would want to complete a career at Virginia Tech, in rural Appalachia – or that I could actually find this sort of career fulfilling. To him, my happiness with Virginia Tech signified a lack of ambition. The natural move would be to seek a trajectory that included UNC–Chapel Hill or Emory before parking finally somewhere in the Northeast.

'I'd rather clean toilets at Virginia Tech than toil in the very pretentious heart of liberal Zionism,' I informed him, only slightly hyperbolically.

A few months later, I encountered a similar attitude from out-of-town guests. Inundated with an apocryphal notion of northern Virginia's appeal, they pressed me out about what my next career move would be. 'You're looking at it,' I smiled. They took it upon themselves to convince me that I couldn't – just *couldn't* – spend my entire career at Virginia Tech. Blacksburg is too small, too isolated. And Virginia Tech's reputation has been made through engineering, not English.

'Woe is me,' I conceded. 'I make decent money. I teach class two days a week and come home by noon on those days. The other part of my job requires me to do what I love to do and what I would do anyway, which is to write. I get to interact in an idyllic atmosphere with smart and lively young people. I declare: I never realized it, but I'm just a step removed from coal mining.' And so I keep hitting the stones, trying my damnedest to avoid crossing the thin line that leads from the ivory tower to a mop, ammonia bottles, and rows of sullied toilets.

My gripe with my concerned friends isn't so much their

declaration of earnest, albeit uninvited, counsel; it is with how they define ambition, which appears to do little more than conform to hegemonic commonplaces. People, academics particularly, often base life and career judgments on superficial things like reputation, which possibly is the most useless criterion because it doesn't necessarily entail the necessity of analytical rigor. Settling into place is a complex process. I'm a nice guy, but I'm not flexible enough to settle into place to somebody else's satisfaction. I welcome others to live out their own ideals about what constitutes quality or desirability.

Needless to say, none of these on-the-spot career counselors is a Virginia Tech graduate. Virginia Tech graduates tend to think of my job as poetically impeccable, which only proves that Tech provided them with a good education.

For an Appalachian boy weary of flat topography, Virginia Tech was an appealing career option. My situation also had the added benefit of a quintessentially American motif: redemption. Having been unable to attend Tech as a student, I found it delectable that I might end up working there as a professor. And unlike most American forms of redemption, mine didn't require any violence. Diana and I managed to exercise ambition peacefully. We beat tremendous odds to end up back in Blacksburg. Finding our way to the Ivy League, state-school pedigree and all, would have been more likely.

The theme of ambition is inscribed so many ways in Virginia Tech. As of April 16, 2007, so is the presence of terrorism.

In so many ways, though, terrorism has remained an unproductive absence. This statement doesn't purport to justify terrorism but to identify its presence; allowing terrorism to remain unidentified renders it absent and thus depleted of meaning. I refer specifically to the morbidly good news circulated by corporate media halfway through April 16, 2007, announcing that the massacre at Virginia Tech was not an act of terrorism. It was merely a massacre, or a killing spree, or a mass murder.

Not identifying the killing spree at Virginia Tech as terrorism is an active omission; that is to say, it is an omission that does lots of things. Identifying the murder of thirty-two innocent people on April 16 as terrorism would not have altered or precluded the fact that it was also a massacre (the two, after all, tend to happen simultaneously). However, referring to the event as terrorism would have added meaning to it. The meanings it would have added are politically inconvenient, and so they were avoided.

Media outlets noted frankly and sincerely that Seung-Hui Cho's violence was not an outbreak of terrorism; newscasters believed what they were saying, and stated this bit of news with no small measure of relief. Had they decided that Cho's rampage was terrorism, they would have concurrently abandoned the extant ideological framework that they use to distinguish terrorism from other forms of violence. The decision to classify the massacre as something other than terrorism was therefore morally layered and politically loaded. If we examine the assumptions underlying the decision, we find that in American usage terrorism must be coterminous with a particular ideology. The identification of this ideology isn't a neutral or natural act. It is one that arises from a series of American geopolitical engagements.

According to corporate media all Arab violence is terroristic, no matter its origin or intent, and so it is reasonable to speculate that if the shooter were an Arab his rampage would have immediately been deemed terrorism. Cho wasn't ideologically vacuous; he in fact articulated an ideology, one incoherently trained on condemning 'rich kids.' Had Cho stated a more explicitly political ideology – the 'particular ideology' to which I refer above – then the interpretation of his act might have changed, especially if Cho had disparaged American foreign policy or some other tin god used to determine an appropriate level of patriotism. Terminological choices in this case indicate that terrorism is usually identified in the United States based on outlook and ethnicity rather than on the actual perpetration of unjustifiable violence, even if it is targeted indiscriminately at civilians.

Even in the absence of a reductive ideological emblem of terrorism, some commentators attempted to find one by locating terrorism in a familiar terrain, a so-called 'Islamic element,' in this case a throwaway signature, 'Ismail Ax,' Cho used on a rambling letter in which he also likened himself – more than once – to Jesus Christ. Ismail, being a Muslim name, potentially rendered Cho's shooting spree terroristic. The self-comparison with Jesus, being ideologically useless, was dutifully ignored.

Let's put this all in perspective. Cho clearly lacked any knowledge or understanding of either Ismail, one of Abraham's sons, or Jesus, one of Abraham's descendants. He composed a screed in a dormitory room between separate mass murders. That it took a cryptic signature referencing nothing other than a delusional allusion for media to contemplate the possibility of an act of terrorism tells us all we really need to know about the arbitrariness of intuition and the politicization of terror. The random murder of thirty-two innocent civilians should have been enough to tip folks off to the possibility of terrorism.

While we're on the subject of terrorism at Virginia Tech, it's important to note that during the coverage of the April 16 massacre corporate media worked hard to disengage all Americana from violence. I heard numerous commentators observe with awe that Cho's family, who are Korean immigrants, seemed to be so well assimilated into the United States. How, then, could one of them do such a thing? This question makes it seem as if violence is absent from the United States and that a true American would never commit violence, or at least not unjustifiable violence. (Cho will never achieve the status of having been a true American.) I would argue, though, that it is precisely because Cho had assimilated that he could do such a thing. School shootings, after all, don't happen in South Korea. They happen in the United States.

Wolf Blitzer performed a similar insinuation in an interview he conducted with Jamal Albarghouti, an international student who had taken a much-aired cellphone video outside of Norris Hall, site of the primary mass murder. Blitzer asked Albarghouti where he is from, a question to which Blitzer already knew the answer. When Albarghouti, a bit confused, answered Palestine, Blitzer asked him to discuss how surprising the violence at Virginia Tech must have been for him. Blitzer was fishing for something specific, for which Albarghouti, perhaps unwittingly, supplied the catch: people in the Middle East are accustomed to violence, and so it must be shocking and maybe even traumatic for them when they encounter violence in the United States.

This line of questioning, common in the aftermath of the shooting, consigns violence to the rest of the world. More important, it ignores the role of the United States in committing and fomenting violence elsewhere. It is a line of questioning that uses ostensible sympathy to disguise a host of jingoistic assumptions. We can pretend with all the smugness available to cultivate our pretension that only foreigners act on violent tendencies. And we can blame rap music and video games for fostering violence until our teeth start to crack. In the end, though, the ugly truth is that the American government does a fine job on its own of nurturing a culture of violence in the United States.

Finally, it's worth pointing out that before Cho had been identified, I heard the following from numerous loved ones: 'I hope he's not an Arab.' Or, after he had been identified: 'Thank God he's not an Arab.' What do these statements mean? How would the tragedy be any different were Cho an Arab?

Nobody who made this statement did so with anything less than complete sympathy; most, in fact, were themselves Arab. Here's how the statement can be interpreted: were Cho an Arab his culture and religion would be used to explain his horrible deed. All Arabs would then be blamed and would be subject to violence, calls for deportation, and/or imprisonment in one of the many secret detention centers in the United States. How do we know this? Because that's exactly what happened to Arab Americans after 9/11. When people said to me, 'Thank God he's not Arab,' they were *really* saying, 'Thank God you're not in danger.'

This tendency to totalize ethnic groups arises from deeply racist impulses in the United States. Whites can commit crimes as individuals, but African, Native, Asian, and Hispanic Americans don't have that option. They commit crimes as symbols of cultural depravity. They're not allowed to act alone. Everything bad that one of them might do is invoked as evidence of group degeneracy. For criminals who happen to be Muslim, there can be no other explanation for their behavior (unless that behavior is favorable).

And so Cho, with his classically un-American appearance, saved media the trouble of practicing introspection.

Yet there's a lucidly human side to the tragedy at Virginia Tech that I am loath to omit. What happened at Virginia Tech is unspeakably ugly. I think about its ugliness as a person who grew up in the vicinity of the campus. My family history ties the act of immigration to an arrival at Virginia Tech. The Virginia Tech campus and the Blacksburg community are engraved in the DNA of my memory. I have a tremendous connection to the place and a profound sense of horror at what happened here. This place binds my existence in the United States to my ancestry in Jordan. But even in moments of tragedy it's important to keep thinking through how tragedy is represented by different folks with different stakes in different forms of representation.

What happened to the students at Virginia Tech isn't terribly different from what happens frequently in Iraq and Palestine. The same is true of other parts of the world, but I want to focus on Iraq and Palestine given the location of my political interests. To be sure, there are serious differences between the massacre in Blacksburg and the typical forms of violence that Iraqis and Palestinians suffer. Therefore, when I say that the two aren't terribly different I'm speaking of the level of fear and terror that routinely is created through violence in Iraq and Palestine. It is at a similar level to what the inhabitants of Blacksburg experienced for the first time on April 16, 2007.

The main difference is that the people in Palestine and Iraq don't have access to the resources of a wealthy and idyllic college campus. They don't have the ability to visit 'round-the-clock counselors.' They can't simply pack up a car and escape. They can't count on the presence of an effective security apparatus. All of these things should have been, and were, available to the Virginia Tech community. They're necessary for all victims of needless violence, and the fact that they're not available to Arab victims of needless violence tells us a lot about how sympathy is prioritized in the United States.

I want Americans to empathize with the violence that Arab victims experience, rather than merely thinking about how the violence they experience affects American interests. I want them to be sorrowful that Israeli occupation soldiers sometimes shoot up Arab schools filled with innocent victims. I want them to understand that what happened in Blacksburg happens every single day in Iraq – sometimes three or four times a day. The people of Iraq have no escape from this horror. On April 16, 2007, 192 Iraqi civilians were massacred. What happened in Blacksburg is harrowing and horrifying and heartbreaking. So is what happens to Palestinian and Iraqi students and civilians, with agonizing frequency. We can condemn the Blacksburg massacre without remorse or atonement. We can grieve without guilt. That's not true of Iraq and Palestine. We're invested in those sites of violence as American taxpayers. We're implicated in them through our indifference.

If the massacre at Virginia Tech doesn't globalize our empathy, then we merely performed a nationalistic ablution in the weeks following the massacre. Tragedies are mitigated when they teach us enduring lessons; they are repeated when we respond to them at surface depth.

On the Sunday following Cho's mass murder, my parents drove to Blacksburg from Bluefield to pay their respects on campus. As if to advertise foreboding or profess symbolism, the weather turned cold and gray the week before April 16. News footage from the morning of April 16 shows snowflakes whisking about in the heavy wind.

This day, though, was beautiful, cloudless and blue and slightly breezy. Buds were in re-bloom. The grass had grown into green fullness. This weather was just as explicitly symbolic.

Accompanied by me and Diana, my parents spent a few hours on campus, reconnecting with an extant presence: as young, ambitious immigrants; as nervous parents moving in a firstborn; as proud, eager photographers at commencement; as aging sweethearts thrilled that one of their children had come home.

Groups of mourning visitors decked out in orange and maroon roamed slowly around the perimeter of the drillfield, stopping at the many posters, tributes, and memorials on display, many of them gifts from universities around the country. There was a much-needed calm on campus because of our collective reverence. There was a comfort in knowing that, at least on this day, we were all in it together. I can't define 'it.' On that day we were simply together. It was a form of camaraderie that I would love to become common. I am as guilty as anybody else that it hasn't been present in the past; I will continue to be guilty if it remains absent in the future.

My parents were entering into the abstract territory of elderly, I realized. My mother was still beautiful, especially on this day, with sunlight adorning a cinnamon skin that had grown only slightly pallid in the aftermath of chemotherapy. The last black hair had left my father's still-thick mane, but he looked dignified in his silver packaging. They walked more slowly these days. They stumbled without having bumped into anything. They rested longer after shorter distances. But they walked together, their hands nestled into one another. They were devastated because of the tragedy. Yet they couldn't help but also be happy. There was no contradiction in these mixed feelings: tragedy engenders togetherness, and happiness arises from nothing other than loved ones coming together.

Diana and I held hands tightly. We could see a trajectory, an alluring future, where we might direct our ambition. This life of ours, we know, wasn't meant to be lived according to the logic of common wisdom. There can be joy in taking the huge risk of seeking the familiar. We aspire to redefine prestige as the consequence of loving one another and staying together. A place like Virginia Tech induces a unique form of serenity.

Those affiliated with Virginia Tech and comparable places don't like to think that violence can so audaciously intrude on our serenity; we are justifiably shocked when it actually does. However, our places exist within broader, violent societies, and troubled youth have to look no further than doctrines of preemption and intervention to learn that a gun emotes more powerfully than dialogue or diplomacy.

The serenity that allows a place like Virginia Tech to be so desirable is worth fighting to preserve. It is worth reproducing. It is, above all, worth exporting. Diana and I have grown intertwined with place in Blacksburg, a multivalent reality. My parents imprinted their passion for us to encounter here. We have become the extension of their past at Virginia Tech. Cho didn't undermine this relationship. He reminded us – at too great a cost – that our serenity always participates in a dialectic with much more brutal ways of being. We should endeavor to remind ourselves of this dialectic without the onset of tragedy.

I am locked into the memory of submitting my job application to the English Department at Virginia Tech. I fit ideally into the position description and adhered already to an ideal about the place where my application was headed. Tech utilized an electronic submission process. I smoked three or four cigarettes in front of the computer, studying and rereading the pdf files that contained my curriculum vitae and cover letter. I couldn't finally bring my index finger to press on the mouse with the cursor positioned atop the 'submit' button. I was certain that I would beat the incredible odds, but nervous that I was falsely brazen. My inner dialogue required me to believe in abstract things like fate or destiny, things I'm not intellectually disposed to consider seriously.

I prepared for my campus visit six months later hours longer than I had ever done for a job interview. Destiny was no longer a consideration. Once I was given an opportunity, I would strive to succeed on my own merit. Neither am I intellectually disposed to failure.

Diana and I had planned out a move to Blacksburg. When I formally accepted a professorship at Virginia Tech, we called my parents in southern Virginia so that we could immediately connect time around its own intricate design. We then called Diana's parents in northern Virginia so that we could immediately connect place to its temporal mission. Over the next few months we moved away from Wisconsin efficiently. We were going home. This move was easy.

Neither of us ever imagined that our first year would be bookended by separate mass murders. Neither of us, however, is inexperienced enough to believe that violence is merely physical. We were surprised, then, in the sense of encountering the unexpected. The violence itself is something that circulates throughout the United States, even in spaces that are free of guns and redolent with belief instead.

The shooting spree on April 16, 2007, was an ambitious form of terrorism, but not uniquely violent. At Virginia Tech it encountered other types of ambition, some empathetic to comparables and others ethnocentric. It has happened before, in so many ways, in so many places. It happened again, somewhere, in some way, even when, on an effulgent spring day, my parents, Diana, and I stopped smiling, unraveled fingers, and stepped over ripples of dried blood baked into a ripened sidewalk.

Is *Jackass* unjustifiable?

O ne of the most wonderful aspects of being a professor is having an opportunity to engage in wide-ranging discussion with bright and insightful students. The most interesting of these discussions focus on the representation of Arabs in American popular culture, which I believe is unjustifiably negative.

It isn't difficult to get a group of people with varying politics to agree that Arabs aren't portrayed favorably in movies and on television. It's the adjective 'unjustifiably' that provokes lively debate. Many of my students, reflecting the viewpoint of most professional commentators, believe that Arabs are portrayed negatively because they deserve to be portrayed that way.

I can understand the rationale of this viewpoint, but nevertheless find it problematic. The portrayal of Arabs as terrorists, fanatics, or just plain shady is unjustifiable not because Arabs have never behaved negatively, but because it's the *only* way

American movies and television portray Arabs. As such, the portrayals collectively imply that Arabs are incapable of contributing anything to American society other than violence or stupidity.

Therefore, when somebody says to me, 'How can films about 9/11 not portray Arabs as terrorists?' I respond by noting that 9/11 is not the only setting in which Arabs can be portrayed. Arabs can be portrayed as doctors, scholars, policemen, scientists, construction workers, devoted parents, and law-abiding citizens. In fact, there is infinitely more of this variety of Arab in the world than there are the two dozen 9/11 terrorists.

The point, in other words, is not to put Irish or Japanese hijackers in the airplanes in movies about 9/11. The point is that Arabs need not be confined to those airplanes because ultimately they are fictitious objects mediated through a story no matter how much they pretend to be real.

Hollywood has an atrocious history of reducing Arabs to idiots and villains. Contemporary agents of anti-Arab racism like *24*, *Hidalgo*, *Jag*, *Fahrenheit 911*, and a passel of campaign commercials have precursors in such classics as *Black Sunday*, *Sirroco*, *Follow That Camel*, and much of the Chuck Norris oeuvre.

The shifty Arab has had a presence in American cinema since the invention of movies.

The argument that acts of Arab terrorism validate these portrayals is causal and rhetorically inadequate. It is also a dubious argument: white Americans commit terrorism, but white Americans are portrayed overwhelmingly as nonviolent.

Conversely, Arabs spend every day *not* committing terrorism but they are rarely portrayed as nonviolent.

Anyway, we are not talking about geopolitical realities. We are talking about representation, which isn't the same thing as reality. Representation, however, often is confused with reality, resulting in what literary theorists call simulacrum, a simulated or alternate reality. And in Hollywood's simulated reality, Arabs aren't allowed to be anything other than terrorists, a situation that renders them rigid exemplars of violence and agents of nothing more.

Therefore, when people argue that it's perfectly proper to constantly reinvent the fictitious Arab terrorist, they are employing an argument that relies on a simulated reality to obscure flawed logic: Arabs are considered to be exemplars of violence not because they commit terrorism in disproportionate numbers, but because they are represented disproportionately as terrorists. The representation, in other words, creates the simulated reality that people then point to as realistic.

I usually suggest to students that I, an Arab American who has never committed violence, should be proof that portraying Arabs exclusively as terrorists is both morally and pragmatically unjustifiable. In this way, my students, who in their lifetimes have only encountered popular-culture Arabs, have access to the reality of Arab life obscured by negative representation.

I like to think that this encounter somehow mitigates the horrible stereotyping of Arabs in today's United States. In some way I'm sure it does. But then again, I've never been in a movie.

*

Is Jackass unjustifiable?

An unlikely exemplar of these issues can be found in *Jackass*, the television-show-cum-movie series featuring stunt men who work hard to justify their self-named moniker. The two *Jackass* films released as of this writing feature a group of young men headed by the campy Johnny Knoxville who perform various stunts or play jokes on one another, with the apparent purpose of causing only slightly controlled pain. *Jackass* is lewd, immature, grotesque, fatuous, and imbecilic.

I consider myself a fan of the series.

I realize that because I'm not a stereotypical frat boy, stoned, or 13 years old I'm not supposed to enjoy *Jackass*, but despite the logical oddity I do. I'm a college professor who wears a sport coat that actually has ovular elbow patches and whose riskiest venture involves bicycling three blocks to Starbucks without a helmet, so I suppose on some level I find something admirable or perhaps envious about people courageous enough to subject themselves to fantastic pain and bodily risk. (One stunt involves three jackasses standing almost naked before a weapon that in one explosion fires a barrage of rubber-coated steel bullets. They end up with bulbous purple splotches on their legs and stomachs. Meanwhile, I shudder at the thought of paper cuts – the subject, incidentally, of another stunt.)

My admiration of the series, though, goes beyond tacit envy or the self-serving detection of an alter ego. I also believe that at certain points *Jackass* unintentionally achieves the status of satire. These points, to be sure, are few and far between, as the series usually remains limited to antics that include some type of anal penetration or another form of barely repressed homoeroticism. And if my conceptualization of the occasional satire as unintentional appears ungenerous it is only because the *Jackass* crew is interested in undermining social conventions, not in satire. The satire happens when undermining social conventions results not merely in the physically absurd but also in a visible critique of conventional absurdity.

In the first *Jackass* movie, for example, Knoxville and company hide in a thicket of pine trees and sound an airhorn – the type used at sporting events, akin to the noise emitted by eighteen-wheelers – as well-heeled golfers tee off. The golfers, predictably, become incensed. One finally flings an iron toward the snickering Knoxville.

I wouldn't argue that this skit is satire, but do believe it contains satirical elements insofar as it completely undermines the trope of gentility so rigidly preserved in upper-class golfing culture. The (self-styled) barbaric Knoxville and his similarly brutish peers force themselves into an unwelcoming, exclusive space and in turn expose its reliance on that exclusivity in order to maintain a spurious prestige, as all restrictive communities throughout history have done. The exclusivity is meant to intimate prestige, but in fact it merely conceals and preserves a deluded self-image. The irony is that because of the filmic profitability of these antics (and his unmistakable whiteness) Knoxville actually could break character and obtain legitimate access to this restrictive space. That he chose to enter it clandestinely adds a layered dimension to the comedy.

Does this example indicate that there is something redeemable about the comedy of *Jackass*? I doubt it. It simply means that there is something funny about it even for the demographic comprised of sober, unduly cautious people.

The climactic skit in *Jackass Number Two* momentarily renders the film an exemplar of issues of representation vis-à-vis Arabs. Titled 'Terror Taxi,' the skit involves a double joke targeted at one of the jackasses, Ehren McGhehey, who is tricked into believing he is playing a joke on a stranger.

McGhehey believes that he is going to pull a racy prank on a random taxi driver who is to transport him to Burbank Airport. McGhehey plans to insinuate to the taxi driver that he is about to commit an act of terrorism. The taxi driver, though, is an actor; the joke will be on McGhehey.

The skit is more scripted than typical *Jackass* offerings and involves a fair amount of planning. McGhehey, first of all, needs to look like a terrorist, the point at which ethnic valuations come into play. In order to accomplish this goal, he is outfitted with a red *kuffiyeh*, sandals, a flowing white robe, a phony dynamite waistband, and a fake beard – this is *Jackass*, after all – constructed without his knowledge from the pubic hairs of the other cast members. He also deploys a phony accent that sounds more like simulated Hollywood Arabic-to-English dialogue than actual ESL speakers from the Arab World. This accent is complete with the inane ranting and chanting that characterize the Arab voice in American media.

From the outset, those involved in the planning of the joke appear tuned into the sort of imagery they employ. 'Do not tell [the cab driver] you are from any particular country,' cast member Preston Lacy impels McGhehey. It is unclear why Lacy delivers this injunction. It may be to usurp potential charges of racism, or it may be to further imbue McGhehey with awareness of the meticulousness required for his mission. Whatever the reason, it indicates a recognition of sensitive words and images.

'It's muffed up, but it's great,' intones another cast member, Bam Margera. Again, it is unclear if Margera refers to the fact that the jackasses are about to cannibalize one of their own with a particularly nasty prank or if he is referring to the type of imagery the prank utilizes. Either way, the statement indicates an awareness of sensitive material that is absent from the other pranks.

The reason that Lacy's and Margera's statements might be conceptualized as more than mere throwaway observations is a corresponding disclaimer that Lacy offers when they are dressing McGhehey as an Arab. 'We're making you look like what we think this guy [the cab driver] expects a terrorist to look like,' he explains. 'We're not making fun of anybody. We're just trying to scare the cab driver.'

The claim 'We're not making fun of anybody' is dubious, even as hyperbole. The jackasses are performing the skit precisely to make fun of people. Lacy was suggesting that the point of the prank isn't to make fun of Arabs or even to stereotype them. The point of the prank instead is to make McGhehey intensely terrified and to induce him to vomit on camera when he finds out that he has motley pubic hair glued to his face. The jackasses deploy an offensive image of Arabs only as a dramatic backdrop to this payoff, which allows Lacy to believe that they're not actually ridiculing Arabs, though he's nevertheless too liberal in his assessment of their intentions.

For his part, McGhehey is up to the role, mouthing idiotic proclamations such as 'I do not like this country, but I do like breasts' from the backseat of the cab and spontaneously intoning the word 'boom' as if he were genetically programmed for terrorism. This portrayal more or less epitomizes how the Arab functions in American movies; at least *Jackass* is marketed as a comedy and makes absolutely no pretension of either quality or insight, as do many films that portray Arabs exactly as 'Terror Taxi' does (*True Lies*, for example, or *The Siege*).

Indeed, I don't think the jackasses are actually trying to make fun of Arabs communally, as an ethnic or cultural group. The show is profoundly anti-communal, in fact, relying on acts of individual courage (or stupidity) in order to generate unaffiliated entertainment. The jackasses are clearly attempting to make fun of their friend McGhehey, but the peculiar dynamics of this particular attempt required the presence of a fake but realistic terrorist.

Thus the inculcation of cultural politics into *Jackass*.

In order to create a simulation of an authentic terrorist the jackasses had to re-create a simulated visage. They in turn employed all the visible markers of Arabness as they have been circulated in popular culture and have come most effectively to signal the presence of a terrorist. These markers are germane to any claim that Hollywood unjustifiably represents Arabs as terrorists because they reproduce a basic flaw: real-life terrorists who have been Arab didn't dress as Arabs; they were simply Arab. That movies feel the need to feature dress symbolizing ethnic positioning in order to highlight cultural predisposition renders the entire enterprise of equating Arabs with terrorism causal and substantially contrived.

This is how it works: say that for Halloween you want to dress as a terrorist. What sort of disguise would you seek? If you answered that you would seek garb that might sartorially represent the corporate boardroom, consider yourself enlightened but squarely in a tiny political minority. Consider also that none of the other party guests would recognize you as a terrorist.

The saddest part of 'Terror Taxi' is that in a sense the jackasses were right: if they were to maximize the possibility of a successful prank by utilizing a costume intended to represent a terrorist, then they had little choice but to evoke stereotypical Arab dress. Our ethical discussion shouldn't be focused merely on the use of the costume, but also on the production of the joke itself, because strategically the jackasses simply responded to the cultural codes with which they are familiar. Those cultural codes dictate that terrorists are best represented by Arabs because Arabs have a monopoly on terrorism.

This fact is an enormously poor reflection not only of Hollywood but of the American politics of representation more broadly. Implicated centrally in those politics is governmental discourse around ethnicity and terrorism. *Jackass* thereby exemplifies the inscription of a specific body politic on symbolic bodies.

'Terror Taxi' would have been much better as a gag were the taxi driver not in on the joke – in other words if McGhehey simply had dressed as an Arab in order to scare an unknowing victim. Given the sensitivity around terrorism in the United States, it would have been nearly impossible to carry out the sort of stunt that McGhehey thought he was carrying out. From this standpoint, the jackasses are implicated in the reproduction of anti-Arab racism through the equation of Middle Eastern imagery with terrorism because they could have played all sorts of nasty jokes on McGhehey without the use of that imagery. By employing terrorism as a central feature of the joke the jackasses consigned themselves to the need for racist imagery as a by-product of particular cultural codes even if the joke doesn't necessarily endorse the morality of those codes.

Even though *Jackass* draws on and thus reproduces these cultural codes, it is the only entertainment institution I know of to acknowledge that it deploys stereotypes and to disassociate itself consciously from those stereotypes concurrent to their deployment. Thus the quintessentially immature and apolitical jackasses are more sensitive to anti-Arab racism than are supposedly high-minded paragons of proper society like Jerry Bruckheimer, Joel Surnow, Ann Hindberg, Arnold Schwarzenegger, and Aaron Sorkin. Interestingly, as Tim Jon Semmerling illustrates in his sterling book *'Evil' Arabs in American Popular Film: Orientalist Fear*, another popular-culture institution to question the veracity of representational commonplaces is the equally raunchy *South Park*.

That only the low-culture *Jackass* and *South Park* seem to be aware of the ridiculousness of ethnic imagery as a political referent tells us something about the ability of self-named high-culture art to regulate its own eminence in order to reproduce endemic racism.

I believe that, as programming, *Jackass* is justifiable. In what context, though, is it justifiable?

It is justifiable because it has a right to be aired. It is justifiable because although it is vulgar and infantile it rarely is offensive. (The same can't be said for many of its more genteel counterparts on the big screen.) It is justifiable because it fills a gap in the pop-culture marketplace.

And, yes, it is justifiable from the standpoint of entertainment value. *Jackass* is strangely funny.

The more interesting question has to do with the content of the series: was the skit 'Terror Taxi' justifiable?

I consider myself attuned to the circulation of negative imagery both subtly and explicitly in movies and on television. With this qualification in mind, I would observe that I don't find 'Terror Taxi' particularly offensive. (This observation should not be mistaken for a claim that 'Terror Taxi' is inoffensive to Arab Americans.) I do find the skit remarkably troublesome, but assign most of the blame to the extant cultural paradigms to which the jackasses merely responded.

In reality, the dramatic equation of Arabs with terrorism is so common that the vast majority of *Jackass Number Two* viewers probably didn't even pay mind to the conditions in which the terror threat could work. 'Terror Taxi' is thus symptomatic of the cinematic and political media in which terrorism is pervasively invested with ethnic identifiers that simulate Arab culture.

It's enough to make me ponder more direct action.

Maybe I should abandon this writing habit and go audition for some movies. *Jackass* seems to require little dramatic training. And I'm certain it's one of the few movie franchises that doesn't engage in racial discrimination. I'll bet that Johnny Knoxville might just be impressed by a sport coat-toting daredevil who bicycles sometimes without a helmet.

The perils and profits
of doing comparative work

I was trained academically as a Native Americanist, a term that I find unattractive, although the term doesn't get much play these days in the field of Native American Studies (or in the many other names Native American Studies goes by or is conflated with: American Indian Studies, Native Studies, Indigenous Studies, Comparative Indigenous Studies, Fourth World Studies). I find the term unattractive because it signals a type of ownership that no scholar has a right to claim either intellectually or ethically. People engaged in Indigenous Studies, as I prefer to call it, tend to identify with communal world-views rather than with empirical or institutional sites of authority. The field rightly demands this sort of orientation these days.

The most appealing thing about doing work in Indigenous Studies is the ability to interact with original peoples everywhere, people who belong to countless national and cultural groups but who nevertheless come together around a set of common aspirations and a worldsense trained on comprehensive justice. It is a field focused not on status but on relations. There are exceptions, of course, and the normal range of individual and geographic taste and style. I am speaking of the ethos of the field, which has evolved into an ardently community-oriented site of interdisciplinarity. In May, 2007, I had an opportunity to attend at the University of Oklahoma (OU) the first gathering of people interested in forming a scholarly Native and Indigenous Studies association. The meeting was vibrant and covered in great detail this sense of community orientation. Once together, it didn't take Native, Maori, Aboriginal, Hawaiian, and Inuit folk long to articulate an ethics of responsibility vis-à-vis the study of Indigenous peoples.

Another appealing dimension of working in Indigenous Studies is the methodological presence of those ethics. Lots of people – Linda Tuhiwai-Smith, Alice Te Punga Somerville, NoeNoe Silva, Dale Turner, Andrea Smith, and many others – are contemplating and utilizing, with vibrant diversity, methodological innovations engaged with traditional ways of knowing and existing. A healthy portion of these innovations think about what it means to conduct work through and within anti-colonial and communal methodologies. Whatever the style or argument each writer or theorist proffers, the ethic across the discipline is that individualistic or disengaged scholarship won't do for Indigenous Studies. This ethic represents an exciting development in academe because it works against a value system that rewards performative reputation and that disinvests inquiry from communities, precluding any lasting responsibility to them beyond the set of ethics that governs research involving humans, which attempts to protect people from being exploited. Protecting humans from exploitation isn't necessarily the same thing as exercising a communal responsibility.

My foray into comparative work began, as all such forays must, with a physical excursion. I figured that if I wanted to study Native literature then I'd better get myself to Indian Country, a space I was lucky to inhabit for seven years. Since I returned to a part of Virginia that doesn't fully qualify as Indian Country, I have been able to revisit Native spaces a few times. Every time I do, I become more honored yet less surprised by the tremendous hospitality and generosity I experience. Indian Country is something of an abstract referent, signifying both geography and world-view, but we should never forget that it is also a concrete domicile whose breadth spans North and South America. There is something spectacularly real about Indian Country, whose realities coalesce around spirit and knowledge. Indian Country, in other words, doesn't merely represent the presence of Natives. It represents ancestral continuity.

When I commenced my comparative work, thinking about ways to put Indian Country into transit was a challenging task. I encountered the same challenges when considering how best to render Palestine itinerant. (Palestine, by the way, occupies an intellectual and geographical location comparable to Indian Country; it is a place both precisely symbolic and ubiquitously real.) I had been enamored of conjoining these two spaces since 1997, when I formally entered into Native American Studies.

I remember finding something vibrant and familiar about the landscapes of Native literature and the tone and tenor of the then-emergent criticism accompanying it. In the ten years since, Native scholarship has been globalized and is the most innovative in the world.

I wanted to render Indian Country and Palestine itinerant because I discovered something tethering them to the same need for movement. I set out to produce an analysis of settlement in the New World and Holy Land. This focus led to the first book I wrote, which was the second I published, *The Holy Land in Transit*. The premiss of the comparison is simple: the settlement of Palestine by European Jews in the late nineteenth and twentieth centuries could not have happened if North America had not been subject to a prior European settlement. The settlement of North America, however, could not have happened without the existence of a mythic Holy Land. Natives and Palestinians, then, were victims of and actors in an identical mythology. The mythology has done lots of things, but its primary quality has been the conferral of divine legitimacy to acts of gross immorality. The mythology, that is to say, has simultaneously inspired and rationalized settler colonization by invoking God's will or by deploying Scripture as a promissory document. In this mythology humans are active in God's affairs, which transforms Him into a weak deity.

When I began developing this work, I was surprised that more writers and scholars weren't investigating the dynamism of that mythology. Hilton Obenzinger, Norman Finkelstein, Robert Warrior, and Sacvan Berkovich had to different degrees explored the transitory disposition of Holy Land mythoi. Other writers – Kathleen Christison, Jace Weaver, Louis Owens, Uri Avnery – had juxtaposed Natives and Palestinians either fleetingly or lucidly, but none had done it systematically. I thought that the Palestinians in particular would be interested in contemplating Native histories in the context of their own dispossession. Israel has been their colonizer, but the United States has been Israel's sponsor – discursively, spiritually, and financially. This fact alone creates an affinity with Natives even if it doesn't on its own produce the groundwork for a scholarly comparison. The Palestinians are still undergoing the atrocious reality of garrison settlement and so they have a strategic interest in developing allies, in addition to acquiring a better understanding of the more abstract predilections that motivate Israel and the United States.

Comparing the discourse of settlement in North America and Palestine initially appears simple: Puritans arrived in what is now New England inundated with messianic fervor. They soon encountered Indians and immediately deemed them Canaanites, Amelkites, Hittites, and other Old Testament tribes, conceptualizing themselves as Israel in the Wilderness and endowing the land with an imagined wealth of milk and honey. In later centuries Americans were overcome by what Obenzinger calls a 'Holy Land mania' that pervaded theology, literature, and politics, ultimately influencing the formation of a modern national identity. The same story traveled back across the Atlantic: European Jews deployed narratives of ancestral belonging as the moral foundation of Zionism and thus recapitulated a mythical relationship with a mystical Holy Land, the promissory site of return. Zionist leaders, including David Ben-Gurion, turned toward the settlement of North America for inspiration as they set out to drain swamps and tame a pristine wilderness sparsely inhabited by premodern savages under whose tutelage the land suffered neglect. In later decades Israel would become an American stronghold in the Arab World, receiving the majority of its foreign aid in addition to its moral and military support.

From this basic but crucial standpoint, comparison is straightforward, as the philosophical rationale for settlement by Euro-Americans and Zionists is analogous and in some ways coterminous. But systematic comparison isn't so simple upon further investigation, especially when we consider the difficulty inherent in serious comparative work of any type. In the case of Natives and Palestinians, who are both colonized populations, we need to orient scholarship – morally and methodologically – toward Indigenous perspectives and when we perform that orientation certain complications arise. These complications are specific to these populations and universal to comparative work in general. The complications furthermore are necessary if any comparison is to reach an acceptable maturity, and so they should be welcomed. But they aren't easy to sort out.

One of the complications is conspicuous: there's not really much the same about Natives and Palestinians. In fact, there's not really much the same about Natives themselves when we look at them properly as hundreds of distinct nations occupying different parts of North and South America. 'Native,' 'Indian,' and 'Native American' are capacious identifiers that are reductionist vis-à-vis actual historical experience; they create a basis for legal categorization and academic study, but they don't do much to illuminate national discreteness and diversity in Indian Country. Adding Palestinians into this hodgepodge amplifies the reductiveness because such an inclusion necessarily privileges the basis of comparison and thus suppresses other equally important phenomena in Native America. This complication is also universal, though: comparison by its nature should be precise; the items of precision achieve privilege because putting two things together is a way of highlighting them and assigning them a special importance.

In comparing Natives and Palestinians, I had to privilege the language of colonial agents and so I ended up, despite my aversion, privileging the agents. In a sense, my work compares the United States and Israel more than it does Natives and Palestinians. Yet I worked hard to make sure that, in keeping with the ethics of Indigenous Studies, my scholarship invested itself into Native and Palestinian intellectual perspectives. This bipolar approach underlines the complexity of performing comparative work. It is difficult to honor a people's space when that space comes into contact with other spaces, however commensurate. When we acknowledge that there's not much the same about different people we limit methodological scope even as we purport to broaden it.

These factors present a series of questions about doing comparative work, which I want to raise and explore in the framework of Native and Palestinian colonization. Does comparative work inherently contravene the ethics of communal investment in Indigenous Studies? Does acknowledging difference among peoples doom comparative approaches or does it sharpen their foci? What do we gain ethically and intellectually when we undertake transnational or cross-cultural comparison? Which possibilities do we sacrifice? How do we conjoin without insinuating or installing homogeneity?

All of these questions partake in a dialectic with a more fundamental one, which I would like to examine here: to what ends should we conduct comparative work?

I want to begin this examination with a caveat: I'm a bit uncomfortable with the word 'should.' Depending on how it's used, it can intimate patronizingly. It can also be employed aggressively as an injunction. Moreover, I'm uncomfortable with its implied finality (though sometimes rhetorical finality is justified). I nevertheless inserted it in the above question rather than 'can' or 'might' because I hope that we will articulate a moral and political program for comparative scholarship, one that needn't be executed in the singular.

We should conduct comparative work to the ends of upheaval and restoration. The best justification for comparative work is also its most desirable outcome: we cannot undermine colonial systems and restore better ways of living in isolation. Comparative work in Indigenous Studies, then, is necessarily activist and proactive. It *should* be engaged in projects of nation-building, not as an injunctive proposition but as a moral exemplar. Indigenous Studies has articulated with remarkable eloquence a series of alternatives to the traditional (and entrenched) notion of the objective and disengaged scholar. These alternatives necessarily cross borders. They have no other choice, anyway, because they de-emphasize borders and epistemologies arising from the colonial metropole. A major impetus of comparative work is to facilitate the orientation of analysis and praxis into Indigenous spaces. This sort of focus allows it to integrate into the project of cultural and political empowerment.

To provide a brief personal example: I would hate for my work not to contribute somehow to the project of undermining Israel. Even if my work doesn't actually change anything on the ground in Palestine I want it to be invested there as a matter of methodological necessity. The ideal underlying my work, in other words, isn't the advancement of scholarly understanding, but the advancement of our ability to understand scholarly complicity in racism and colonization. The work can then realistically rather than disingenuously effectuate ideals of scholarly responsibility. It can only do so, however, through fruitful contextualization. How can we properly understand Israel if we don't properly understand the United States? We cannot properly understand the United States if we ignore its genocidal origins. Comparison, in this case, arises from and leads back to the interrelation of colonial power with paradigmatic discourses of chosenness and altruism.

Comparison can be fruitful for other reasons. Transnational comparativists fear reducing Indigenous peoples to whatever happens to be the basis of comparison, in the case of Natives and Palestinians their experience of being colonized. Both Natives and Palestinians, though, are much more than victims of colonial perfidy. They existed well before the onset of colonization and they continue to exist outside of its reach and influence. Natives participate in profoundly rich cultural, social, and spiritual practices, and they have done so since the beginning of their existence. Palestinians have been rooted in the Holy Land since the time when the landscape had yet to be invested with a textual sanctity. They too exist before and beyond Israel's presence.

To undertake a comparative analysis of colonization in North America and Palestine, then, is to subsume Natives and Palestinians in the lexicon of foreign settlement, quite like the space where they often are confined politically. This reality is problematic because it limits an engagement with myriad cultural and historical phenomena. The trade-off, however, ultimately makes the limitation worthwhile. If we choose to abjure the limitation, we concurrently abandon comparative work in general because the precision comparativists pursue inevitably engenders circumscription.

Anyway, scholarship, like writing generally, always involves trade-offs. Reasonable people don't write to shut down conflict or to shut out complexity. The skilled among us write to transmute obvious into complex and to elide the innocuous. Something invariably is traded aesthetically or rhetorically when we commence to produce meaning through the act of writing. If we endeavor to compare, then we trade the ability to be adequately comprehensive. If we endeavor to be adequately comprehensive, then we trade the ability to be effectively comparative.

Through comparison, we might experience the benefit of learning about ourselves. Less obliquely, I mean to say that folks rationalize comparison as a way to engage and better understand other cultures, traditions, and geographies. This rationale is a fine reason to pursue comparative work, and broadening one's knowledge of peoples and places is a reasonable ambition. We can also look at comparison as a self-edifying undertaking. I don't mean to suggest an undertaking that is visibly or implicitly selfish. I am suggesting instead that there is something remarkably valuable about contemplating community in a collectivist environment. Thinking about what it means to belong to a particular group with cultural practices, historical narratives, and geopolitical engagements is most fruitful when we welcome others into the process. For example, in March, 2007, on *Democracy Now!* Eli Painted Crow, a Yaqui who had served as an army sergeant during the war on Iraq, revealed that American military officials referred to enemy territory as 'Indian Country.' This revelation, which also was made public during the invasion of Vietnam, is shocking in its ideological connotations and unmistakably connects an imperialist past to the present. Painted Crow was able to contextualize the war on Iraq within broader understandings of colonization that became self-edifying because they extended her range of analysis.

This example illuminates another beneficial feature of comparison, which is the ability it gives us to create new intellectual paradigms. Participants in the OU conference examined with various outcomes this potential feature of inter-communal scholarship. An issue of general agreement is the need to work beyond physical and conceptual boundaries, which are inherited from European (read: colonial) systems of knowledge. The very idea of creating a professional site of Indigenous Studies is fundamentally transnational. The new paradigm of primary interest is methodologically national- ist, which would seem to disaffirm comparative emphases. In the context of Indigenous Studies, however, a nationalist methodology describes more than anything an intellectual and ethical orientation in communal polities and, correspondingly, a shift away from objective and positivistic epistemologies. To profess a nationalist identity is simultaneously to commit to an international group of communities rather than to any nation- state. These communities, sometimes referred to collectively as the Fourth World, acknowledge a commonality of interests as Indigenous peoples.

An interesting result of that commonality might be the possibility of using comparative work to create a basis for political alliance, even if this alliance would remain hypotheti- cal. The idea of using scholarship to inform political work in itself represents a serious departure from traditional academic ethos, which maintains the erstwhile myth of disinterest. This myth is troublesome for four main reasons: (1) it suggests that proper academics can achieve a transcendent eminence that allows them to eschew politics; (2) it assumes that eschewing politics is a good thing; (3) it renders 'political' a coded word that can identify for the elite anything perceived as threatening or undesirable; and (4) it perpetuates the lie that only people of color are political, or, inversely, the lie that white professors only impart objective knowledge. In fact, asserting a nonpolitical orientation is a highly political act – I use 'political' here to reflect the same deprecating manner in which the ostensibly nonpolitical use the term.

The development of political work through scholarship shouldn't be seen as unprofessional or didactic. In Indigenous Studies, the incorporation of communal and activist needs – that is, 'political' things – into scholarly analysis has been done with great sophistication. (See the work of Robert Warrior, Winona LaDuke, Vine Deloria, Jr., Inez Hernandez-Avila, J. Kehaulani Kauanui, Maylei Blackwell, or just about anybody else aligned with Native and Indigenous Studies.) Exploring transnational and inter-ethnic alliances, intellectual and activist, would be a normal extension of any belief that research should be communally invested. We can already see exciting connections emerging among Pacific nations and even more comprehensively through extensive inter-hemispheric dialogue. In this age of mass communications, it is easy – necessary, one could argue – to move intently away from colonial epistemologies and instead to advocate, through scholarship, for the restoration of full Indigenous nationhood.

We have to think about the impetus for comparative work within the concept of hegemony, even if it makes us sound more cynical than we probably are. Who benefits from the ethic that scholarship must remain disengaged? The beneficiaries, of course, are those who profit from supposedly disengaged scholarship (and from a disengaged citizenry in general).

Indigenous peoples of all nationalities share a basic interest in claiming ownership of their own value systems. That interest extends to the need to incorporate those value systems into the way they conduct and present research.

I advocate comparative work most avidly around the potential it creates for political collaboration, although intellectual collaboration is highly appealing and indivisible from the political. These categories, in any case, don't make much sense and only retain their use based on a decidedly politicized, albeit supposedly neutral, Western taxonomical paradigm. In this taxonomy, the political becomes anything that threatens the status quo. It is for this reason that I deem the political in Indigenous Studies coterminous with useful intellectual work. I don't want to encourage the retention of binaries, but there is no way to evolve Indigenous Studies in an acceptable fashion without threatening the academic status quo. Indigenous Studies will invariably be pegged with the label of political wherever it arises, as it is wherever it has already been established. Indigenous peoples have strength in their intellectual vision, however, and they increasingly have demographic strength. If the emergence of comparative work can link various communities into a common set of ambitions, then it will be one of the rare instances in which scholarship actually performs a vital role in the world and influences more than two dozen people.

There are no easy ways to get different communities together and to articulate a common set of ambitions, and so I'm loath to become too optimistic, but people often confuse a goal's feasibility with its ethical value, which seems to me a way of putting the cart before the horse. Just because it may be difficult – potentially impossible – to do these things doesn't mean that we shouldn't invoke the goal to instruct our methodological ethics. Even as a methodological principle, comparative work runs into the problem of reduction and so it's important to articulate an honest critique of how Indigenous communities recoup what they sacrifice and why (if) crossing cultures is worth its promise. The particular challenge is to make Indigenous communities mobile while allowing them to remain proudly discrete.

Now might be a good time to shift direction for a moment. Surely somebody reading this essay has wondered, 'Who is Indigenous? Who is Salaita speaking about in this essay?' This is an important question, one that needs to be answered but one that is remarkably vexing. If the goal is to bring Indigenous peoples together through comparative scholarship, inter-communal activism, and a professional association, then, to paraphrase Te Punga Somerville, who should be on the guest list? I would add the following to Te Punga Somerville's metaphor: who gets to compose and distribute the guest list? The first problem we encounter in considering these questions is the fact that an Indigenous Studies ethic would reject normative ethnicity or authenticity. Nobody should hypothetically be in a position to create a guest list, nor should anybody hypothetically have the moral authority to exclude people from it.

Yet beyond the hypothetical, Te Punga Somerville is absolutely correct. People do need to be invited just as certainly as others need to be excluded. This need, after all, is the entire basis of separating from extant professional associations and forming one by and for Indigenous peoples. Likewise, we cannot think usefully about comparative work without at least implicitly judging who is worthy of comparison. This situation is rather stouter than a paradox; it is more akin to a philosophical apparatus, one whose various resolutions present tacit directives.

I would like to evoke the spirit of Robert Warrior's *Tribal Secrets*, where he encourages us to avoid cumbersome questions about identity and belonging. It's never a good idea to spend lots of time debating categorical questions, even if those questions appear to be of paramount import. Shifting discussion into more tangible items isn't necessarily the same as shirking those difficult questions. Rather, it is a methodological decision to be confident in the assertiveness of Indigeneity as an organic and political identity and to acknowledge that questions of authority and authenticity cannot be answered satisfactorily; to invoke them repeatedly ends up benefiting the same dominant culture that assigned them importance in the first place. A shorthand ethic about the guest list can merely note that an Indigenous community is one that identifies itself as such and one that is accepted as such by its brethren.

I realize that this answer is unsatisfactory and that it doesn't adequately address my own assertion that people do need to be included and excluded. I would add that Indigeneity is naturally and necessarily intangible and so it can never be defined, even as a broad referent, using the logical conventions of Western scholarship, or even through basic linguistic communication. It is defined by the way that people identify themselves, their families, and their communities; how they relate to other humans and the world; the type of respect they offer living things; the way they choose to honor what came before them; how worldsense is inherited and imparted. Indigeneity, that is to say, is a practiced identity; it's not a political category that can be outfitted with manifest criteria. People belong to the category by participating in communities that are indigenous to the worldly places that actualize Indigeneity. I am speaking in this essay, then, about those who call themselves Indigenous without ever having considered a set of criteria to quantify that identity.

The entire process of inclusion and exclusion needs to be self-regulating. Even if this option is flawed, it is less flawed than its alternatives, which are all to some degree deterministic.

I can also answer the question of inclusion and exclusion through discussion of a specific example: are Palestinians Indigenous? I raise this question in *The Holy Land in Transit* and conclude that, yes, insofar as Palestinians comprise a people invested in a particular landscape, they are Indigenous. I also argue that Palestinians are politically Indigenous insofar as we use the term to designate a colonized or dispossessed people who have a legitimate claim to land usurped by a foreign occupier. Both geographical rootedness and the experience of colonization are germane to an Indigenous identity, but they aren't the only things that create or define one. Within Palestinian society itself, for example, there are communities – primarily the Bedouin of the Naqb Desert – distinguishable as Indigenous from the rest of Palestinian society. They are distinguished as Indigenous based mainly on their traditional lifestyle and its attendant manifestations: housing, mobility, dress, worldsense, family structure, dialect. Mostly, though, the Bedouin are known to be Indigenous because they practice a life of Indigeneity. When we add Israel back into the equation, it renders the rest of Palestinian society Indigenous in that Palestinians are forced to profess a subject position that invests the Holy Land with their cultural and historical presence. This type of profession is a foundational expression of Indigeniety.

To backtrack slightly: yes, I would think that Palestinians belong on the guest list, though they are not an obvious choice, as do Iraqis and the many tribal or nomadic peoples of the Arab World who are displaced by the state for various reasons (to usurp farmland, to expropriate resources like oil or water, to construct public works projects such as dams, and so forth). The guest list should also include all communities around the world whose identity is created by and invested in places that become even more sacred vis-à-vis corporate incursions in collusion with the state. These folks live in South and Central Asia, Latin America, sub-Saharan Africa, Eastern Europe, the South Pacific – everywhere, really, where there are corporate interests that can only be implemented through environmental and cultural extirpation. Thus the power that binds us together: Indigenous peoples are the ones who most ardently and consistently reject corporate modernity but who nevertheless can indirectly affect its success – and can directly effect its demise.

If Indigenous scholarship can't or won't contribute to this project, then there's no need to designate it as 'Indigenous.' Without this mission, it won't really have anything to do with the communities to which it affixes itself. And without utilizing cultural traditions and conventions in order to produce scholarly meaning, the work loses the ethical and methodological distinctiveness that enables it to be Indigenous. Indigenous scholarship, therefore, is fundamentally seditious, and it is intrinsically comparative. Yes, there are perils to doing this kind of work – but what we respond to, together, with sundry vision, is far more perilous.

What is Michael Lerner
really talking about?

Because of his gravitas among American liberals, Rabbi
Michael Lerner, founder of the Tikkun Community and
editor of its publication, *Tikkun Magazine*, has gained access
to a number of prominent left-liberal outlets. Indeed, only
the Arab or Muslim Americans who disavow Islam and Arab
cultures through admiration of Israel (Irshad Manji, Fouad
Ajami, Nonie Darwish) have access to an audience as broad
as Lerner's.

This fact is no accident. Beyond some forums on what might
be called the hard left, Arab voices are largely absent from
non-Arab media. We are rendered invisible as agents of our own
narratives because people already are narrating on our behalf:
liberal and progressive Zionists, who have come to represent
the 'anti-Israel' position vis-à-vis 'pro-Israel' commentators
(drawn from the ranks of those who never admit to Israeli

wrongdoing, such as Alan Dershowitz, Charles Krauthammer, Daniel Pipes, and so forth).

First of all, we should note that these categories of 'pro-Israel' and 'anti-Israel' are stupid. They make no sense even as shorthand referents and in fact are implicitly pernicious because they equate the pursuit of justice (i.e. condemnation of Israel) with irrationality or blind hatred; the descriptor 'anti-Israel' emphasizes an inherent or inherited antipathy and implies that one objects to Israel *ipso facto* rather than to Israel's objectionable behavior, a decidedly admirable position. It would be more useful to categorize people according to their moral stances – for example, 'in support of human rights,' as against, perhaps, 'an apologist for Israeli ethnic cleansing.'

The categories also are explicitly pernicious because they have been constructed in such a way that Arabs are almost completely excluded from them. In a long conflict that has pitted Israeli Jews against Palestinian Arabs, one would think that debates about the conflict would include both Jews and Palestinians. Instead, the Palestinians have been replaced by liberal and progressive Zionists who, like their ostensible adversaries, refuse to interrogate the discourses underpinning the divine foundations of Israel and rarely move beyond weak liberalist critiques of the state's origin and its ensuing (and continuing) brutality. These liberal and progressive Zionists therefore do not actually represent the Palestinians on whose behalf they pretend to speak. They do a much better job of unwittingly, and in some cases knowingly, representing Israel's interests than they do an interest in peace and justice.

The same is true, incidentally, of white liberals relative to all ethnic groups around the world facing some form of oppression. The most obvious test case for this assertion is the relationship among white liberals and North America's Indigenous peoples. White liberals, in sadly overwhelming numbers, dutifully ignore or sanitize the multiple histories of genocide endured by Natives during the long process of nation-formation in the United States. The ignorance and sanitization are themselves detestable, but are rendered fully abhorrent only when we recognize the complicity of today's white liberals in continued forms of Native displacement, dispossession, and cultural genocide through the corporate desecration of sacred geography and the continued abrogation of various treaty rights.

White liberals, then, have a poor record of decolonial advocacy. In fact, colonization wouldn't have lasted fifteen minutes anywhere in the world were it not for the acquiescence of liberals in the metropole. (See the 2003 American invasion of Iraq for a fine example.)

For this reason, liberal and progressive Zionists aren't merely timid politically. It would be unwise for Palestinians to let them off the hook by deeming them good-hearted but a tad naive. They play a fundamental role in the capacity of colonizers to invent a rationale for inexpiable barbarity by normalizing through discursive quiescence the state apparatuses that foreground and depend upon the suppression of Indigeneity, except in the moments when it can be appropriated to legitimize a foreign colonial presence. They play a more crucial role on Israel's behalf by preventing Palestinians from entering into the spaces of public debate where their viewpoints and narratives rightly belong – and which are rightly feared by liberal and progressive Zionists, who cannot imagine a form of Arab empowerment that does not conform to the impotent political boundaries they have so meticulously erected. As a result, the Israel–Palestine conflict becomes a Jew-on-Jew issue devoid of Arab participation, thereby reinforcing the racist paradigms that privilege Jews as rightful stewards of the Holy Land in addition to the many issues permeating it.

Let's return to Michael Lerner, the progressive Zionist par excellence and go-to commentator for liberal media seeking an oppositional voice. He serves a necessary function for such media – including the *New York Times* – because he saves them the trouble of having to feature a Palestinian who might accurately identify the ugliness of Israel's past and present.

Lerner prefers to highlight what he deems both Israeli and Palestinian immorality and discusses the two parties as if there is historical and political equivalency between their deeds. He also reliably sanitizes the viciousness of Israel's creation and couches his moral critique in a framework that minimizes Palestinian suffering by highlighting what he conceptualizes as their excessive terrorism.

For example, in his commentary about Israel's devastation of Lebanon, which he calls a 'pointless round of violence' and an 'episode in irrationality,' Lerner writes,

> Within the context of blame, there's enough to go around. It all depends on where you start the story. Counting on lack of historical memory, the partisans on all sides choose the

place that best fits them into a narrative in which they are the 'righteous victims' and the others are the evil aggressors. Palestinians like to start the story in 1948 with the expulsion of hundreds of thousands of Palestinians from their homes during the war on Israel proclaimed by neighboring Arab states, and the refusal of the Israeli government to allow these people to return once the hostilities ceased. Israelis prefer to start the story when Jews were desperately seeking to escape from the genocide they faced in Europe, and a cynical Arab leadership convinced the British military to side with local Palestinians who sought to prevent those Jewish refugees from joining their fellow Jews living in Palestine at the time.

Lerner tells the same story in his book *Healing Israel/Palestine* and likes to repeat it in essays and public appearances. The story is despicable not merely because of its historical inaccuracy and its reduction of garrison colonization to a misunderstanding-gone-wrong, but because he also assigns blame for the origin of the conflict not to the Jewish ethnic cleansers but to their Palestinian victims. He accomplishes this inversion by condemning Palestinians for not opening their country to Jewish settlement, forgetting, of course, that Palestinians had nothing to do with the Holocaust and that Zionism, which always desired to cleanse the land of Palestinians, is a pre-Hitler phenomenon.

(Lerner, incidentally, scolded Edward Said – after Said's death, in keeping with Lerner's moral intrepidness – for not having sympathized properly with European Jews returning to 'their ancient homeland.')

Lerner has a long history of condemning Israel by upbraiding Palestinians for their selfishness. In a 2002 op-ed in *The Nation*, for instance, he admonishes 'pro-Palestinian groups that claim the Palestinians are facing Nazi-like genocide at the hands of the Jewish people' and calls for 'reconciliation between two peoples who share equally the blame for the current mess.' The saddest part of this pronouncement, beyond the frequency with which Lerner repeats it, is its dehumanization of Palestinians by reducing their long and courageous resistance to the same class of immorality entailed by a hundred years of Zionist ethnic cleansing.

Upon Israel's invasion of Lebanon, Lerner ostensibly condemned Israel without actually criticizing it. He assembled fifty-three signatories to an advertisement that ran in the *Los Angeles Times* and the *New York Times*. The first condition for peace that Lerner articulates includes 'the full and unequivocal recognition by Palestinians and the State of Palestine and all surrounding Arab states of the right of Israel to exist as a Jewish state.' To Lerner, peace is coterminous with preserving Israel's Jewish majority – that is, its right to be institutionally racist by remaining legally ethnocentric. Rather than calling for the right of return, a prerequisite for any lasting peace, Lerner champions 'generous reparations,' thus ensuring continued disenfranchisement for millions of refugees and proffering a type of liberal altruism that has caused the Palestinians and all other colonized peoples incalculable suffering for over a hundred years. The entire ad never rises above the inanity of liberal platitudes.

It is worth noting that of the fifty-three signatories in Lerner's advertisement, only two appear to be Muslim, one of whom is Arab (an Iraqi). No Lebanese or Palestinian is represented.

These embarrassing demographics are in keeping with another widely circulated letter headlined by Noam Chomsky and signed by eighteen luminaries, none of whom is Arab or Muslim. Lest a racist impulse compel one to wonder if famous Arab writers were omitted because there are none, it's difficult to imagine that nobody had the foresight to contact Naomi Shihab Nye, Ahdaf Soueif, Leila Ahmad, Nawal El Saadawi, Mahmoud Darwish, Adonis, Nathalie Handal, Etel Adnan, Salma Khadra Jayyusi, Amin Maalouf, or Hanan Al-Shaykh.

Perhaps it's for the best that Lerner offered a statement about Israel, Lebanon, and Palestine that omitted Lebanese and Palestinians, because those voices do not belong with him; they are much more useful if unburdened from Lerner's brand of moral diffidence. He does little more than peddle nonsense and recruits lots of famous people who should know better but nevertheless come aboard because they accept Lerner's supposed benevolence or because Lerner appeals to their upright self-image without getting them into any real trouble, as a close association with Palestinians surely would.

One senses in Lerner's writing a devoted ideological Zionist tussling with the genteel ideology of multicultural coexistence; the multiculturalist in Lerner manages to produce a sheen of tolerance, but close readings of his work always reveal the ethnocentric zealot.

Lerner also fancies himself a leader of Palestinians. This conceit is articulated in his 2002 *Nation* op-ed, where he encourages his readers to make 'demands on Jewish and Arab institutions to adopt a path of nonviolence.' I would urge Lerner to make whatever demands on Jews that he wishes to make, but notify him that he has no right to make any demands on the Palestinians. And if the readers he addresses also are progressive Zionists (or any type of Zionist) then they likewise have no right to do anything vis-à-vis the Palestinians but to clean the stink from their own houses rather than transporting that stench into the homes of others.

Lerner emblematizes the failings of white liberals engaged with colonial dynamics in the same manner as the character Susan Barton in J.M. Coetzee's superb fictive meditation on South African apartheid, *Foe*. Thinking of Friday, the slave reimagined in *Foe* as a black man whose tongue purportedly has been cut out, Susan can't help but encounter a brief moment of lucidity:

> 'I tell myself I talk to Friday to educate him out of darkness and silence. But is that the truth? There are times when benevolence deserts me and I use words only as the shortest way to subject him to my will. At such times I understand why Cruso preferred not to disturb his muteness. I understand, that is to say, why a man will choose to be a slaveowner. Do you think less of me for this confession?'

With this scene, Coetzee has performed a fantastic rhetorical maneuver. Susan either hopes or imagines that her momentary honesty might warrant sympathy, as acts of honesty tend to do for those who volunteer them. Yet this momentary honesty actually implicates Susan as immoral in opposition to the benevolent self-image she has worked so hard to cultivate and project through her written discourse.

Lerner is quite like Susan Barton, without any moments of lucidity or the occasional honesty.

I affirm Lerner's right to his discourse, no matter how insidiously dangerous it is. Lerner, however, should never claim that he represents the viewpoints or the interests of the Palestinians. He does not. By whitewashing Israel's founding, repeatedly calling for the maintenance of a racist ethnocentric state, and conceptualizing himself as a Zionist, Lerner ultimately represents a position of power that he never will be willing to abandon.

It would be wise for Palestinians and those who truly care about their well-being therefore to abandon Michael Lerner.

Immigrants are not homogenous

I was in another gawky phase then: fifteen, lanky, and slightly knobby-kneed, with new swarthy body hair covering old tawny skin, a turbid black '*do* extending my height by four inches, all complemented by marbled plastic eyeglasses.

It was early 1991. The grand maple trees in our large Appalachian backyard were denuded, transformed by winter into desultory sticks clicking against one another in the periodically heavy wind. The once-verdant lawn took on a matted appearance, resembling champagne in complexion, but without any of its celebratory overtones. Our redbrick ranch, outstretched by a recent addition, wasn't necessarily cozy but was secure, a space where electric baseboard heaters emitted warmth with a persistent clack.

We liked to gather around the television during winter evenings, in a room that fit five perfectly: snugly enough to suggest genuine togetherness, but with space to stretch into individual postures. In those days the only thing to watch was the newly launched American invasion of Iraq, the first multimedia war. We even got to watch the CNN feed in second-period algebra and during lunch study.

We all knew that Saddam Hussein was evil personified, his smirking mug emblematic of Arab irascibility, his thick mustache not so much a personal adornment as a symbol in the Western imagination of burly, impenetrable difference. It was sixteen years before he dangled from a rope on YouTube. He would survive this war. Millions of Iraqi people would not.

At school, my peers treated the war like a video game, cheering and whistling when television stations proudly reran high-tech graphics showing air missiles hitting their targets, ambiguous beige squares with a big X implanted on them before streaking gray lines reduced them to puffs of smoke. None of us ever considered – were ever led to consider – that people, actual humans with fingers and toes, inhabited those ambiguous gray squares. At home, my parents were less enamored, shaking their heads slowly, occasionally offering a grunt through pursed lips.

I wasn't particularly clamorous, but I was a healthily curious teenager. I loved books and spent most of my time, inside and outside of class, reading anything I could get my hands on, in any genre. I delighted in both Archie comics and Charles Dickens, treating the two as nothing more than competing visualizations of basic human relationships. I hadn't yet taken to writing, but was starting to develop an instinct for identifying good work. My mind was inattentive to scholastics, but active. I wasn't the stereotypically apathetic and hormonal teenager.

And I knew that I had a slightly different rooting interest than fellow Appalachians in the war. That is to say, I knew that I wasn't merely an American. I was also an Arab, like the Iraqis. Like Saddam Hussein.

This reality wasn't lost on my classmates, who routinely demanded that I reaffirm my loyalty to the United States. The best way to express that reaffirmation was to pump my fist along with everybody else when American warplanes blew things up. The need for self-preservation notwithstanding, I somehow felt like a traitor in such moments, though I understand now that my actions weren't traitorous, but immoral, something I didn't consider at the time.

But it was difficult to engage the multimedia war with any sort of emphasis on morals. If one didn't actively choose to think about the Iraqis dying from airstrikes, then one never had to think about them. They were completely absent from the fancy graphics and the expert analysis. It didn't feel like we were viewing something serious, like a war; we had an abstract sense instead that we were watching a continuous movie. Saddam was the ubiquitous villain.

My classmates said that I resembled Saddam. We both had black hair and the same skin color, something of a high olive; these two factors – themselves not necessarily similarities – were adequate for most people to conceptualize us as identical, or close enough. It was becoming harder and harder to ignore what was symbolized by this supposed resemblance: the fact that I was Arab, a fact understood by my classmates, one simply articulated, as Americans are trained to do, through a critique of appearance.

There were whispers about a draft. I first heard them from my friend's mother, who fretted that her bald, hobbled husband, a Vietnam War veteran, would be called into combat again. Members of the senior class at school also discussed the possibility, the college-bound wondering if an acceptance letter would qualify them for exemption, the military enlistees even more excited, as they boasted, to go 'kick their ass and take their gas.' Sure, we were whupping Saddam, but nobody knew when the war would end. I was less than three years away from draft eligibility. What if I, an Arab, were forced to go to the Middle East to kill other Arabs?

Looking back, I realize that my quandary was unnecessary, based on a melodramatic premiss. At the time, though, it presented a moral dilemma that I couldn't quite work out, one of many immigrant quandaries unique to the United States. One evening, as the multimedia war endured, to the apparent delight of the broadcasters, I decided to ask my parents what they thought.

'You're an American,' my mother offered, without hesitation. 'If you're called to fight for your country, you do it, no matter what and no matter where.'

'Bullshit,' my father replied.

Distress and bluster at Columbia; or, The day Mahmoud Ahmadinejad was invited to academe and promptly emblematized terrorism

In September 2007, Iranian President Mahmoud Ahmadinejad traveled to Columbia University to deliver a speech as a guest of the School of International and Public Affairs. Both the invitation and the subsequent appearance generated predictable controversy. Ahmadinejad's objectionable statements and his questionable domestic policies were only the superficial bases of the controversy, though. Many American universities, after all, host tyrants, dictators, and other unsavory types, treating them as honorable guests in spaces free of anything but marginal disputation (King Abdullah, Pervez Musharraf, Henry Kissinger, Benjamin Netanyahu, and George W. Bush come to mind). Controversy around Ahmadinejad, then, only makes sense in a particular geopolitical context; claims of his dubious behavior are too selective to be taken seriously as anything other than a rationalization for the controversy. Ahmadinejad's visit to Columbia generated protest because of his metonymical attributes, particularly his emblematization of Holocaust denial and terrorism (more systemic as calls for invading Iran grow stronger). Many of those who protested constantly seek an excuse for hawkishness and do not miss an opportunity for complaint. Ahmadinejad's visit was a blessing for those who seem to know how to do little else but clamor for war.

My point here isn't to absolve Ahmadinejad of leadership failures, which American media have carefully documented (and exaggerated). My point is to ask readers to think about the conditions in which one unsavory figure can inspire hysteria and come to emblematize unjustifiable violence while equally unsavory figures merely inspire apathy or indifference. The more interesting move is to think about the conditions in which unsavory figures come to inspire reverence (Ronald Reagan, Hosni Mubarak, and Shimon Peres come to mind). Condemning Ahmadinejad and screaming about his evil is the intellectual equivalent of banging a spoon to a pan, and the moral equivalent of pumping gas into an Abrams tank. If his visit symbolized to Americans the epitome of villainy and set off a debate about domestic institutions such as free speech, then that visit deserved to have been examined analytically. Basic analysis illustrates that more than anything Ahmadinejad's speech at Columbia mobilized the tacitly jingoistic sentiment underlying American humanism. Ahmadinejad is only important insofar as Americans need someone to embody foreign policy anxieties. As a human agent or a participant in world politics Ahmadinejad is nearly irrelevant; he is much more useful to Americans as an invention of their own racist disposition.

But this essay isn't actually going to be about Mahmoud Ahmadinejad (just as Mahmoud Ahmadinejad's visit to Columbia wasn't actually about Mahmoud Ahmadinejad). It will be about the metonymical factors underlying Ahmadinejad's invitation and his subsequent mistreatment by Columbia University President Lee Bollinger and corporate American media. Bollinger assumes the mantle of both free-speech expert and advocate, but his actions belie the image. His refusal in 2006 to speak in defense of faculty under attack by a group of well-funded Zionists was more indicative of pusillanimity than integrity. When he exploited the occasion of the speech to lecture Ahmadinejad about civil rights and discourse, he rendered himself a blustery hypocrite. We needn't invoke Bollinger's ostensible free-speech advocacy to proffer this observation; it can be observed by turning our attention to Bollinger's own president, whom Bollinger has never lectured. Ahmadinejad has never made an objectionable statement or performed an inhuman act unmatched by Bush's words and deeds. Indeed, if we ignore the realm of discourse (which is important, but not as important as praxis) and focus instead on action, then Bush is an eminently more dangerous leader than Ahmadinejad. Until Bollinger has something to say to Bush – not merely about him, but *to* him, in public – then his criticism of Ahmadinejad was nothing other than grandstanding.

The context of this grandstanding includes widespread American xenophobia and Islamophobia. On the stage at

Columbia, Ahmadinejad entered into sanctified space as the stranger, a swarthy emblem of inalterable alterity. It is through this fixed difference that Americans could smugly avoid seeing Bollinger's soapbox oration to Ahmadinejad as a projection of their own depravity. Americans have been trained since 1979 to preclude Iranians from the same level of humanity they assign to themselves. This process is varied and it can be both subtle and explicit. An example of its frequent subtlety arose from CBS Evening News anchor Katie Couric, who, according to *New York Times* columnist Maureen Dowd, remembers how to pronounce Ahmadinejad's name with the mnemonic device 'I'm a dinner jacket.' This idiotic strategy, predicated on a mispronunciation, doesn't bespeak racism directly, but it does indicate a lack of intercultural seriousness, an attitude that allows racism to circulate beyond those who are racist. No attempt is made – no attempt needs to be made – to explore Iranian history, culture, and language outside of their uses as shadow entities in American doctrines of intervention.

If we situate the Ahmadinejad imbroglio within an analytical framework that accounts for important metonymical phenomena, then we will discover some useful things about the utility of the Muslim Other in today's American sense of individual strength and nationhood. Three things in particular become apparent in the discourse of American civility, which is both exceptionalist and latently racist (in those instances when its racism is not explicit): (1) Arabs and Muslims understand only violence as a form of interchange and are completely stupid around questions of progress and enlightenment; (2) the accusation of an absence of civil and human rights in the Muslim World grows in frequency and loudness in direct proportion to the erosion of civil and human rights in the United States; and (3) the complex process of image-making in the United States invests what would otherwise be mundane or unremarkable visual items of Arabic culture with sinister connotations. Let's take a closer look at each of these observations.

The notion that Arabs and Muslims cannot be reasoned with using conventional forms of dialogue and must therefore be forced through violence into subordinate positions has gained in popularity. That notion has existed for some time in the American lexicon, but it was mainstreamed upon commencement of the second Palestinian intifada in September, 2000. The impetus for its popularity is the opportune theory that Israel must forcibly subdue the Palestinians for two main reasons: to teach them that violence will be returned in kind and to enter into negotiations from a position of power. This theory has most adamantly been advanced by Middle East Forum director Daniel Pipes. Just before having become an adviser to the Rudy Giuliani presidential campaign, Pipes observed that he has

> called for shutting off utilities to the Palestinian Authority as well as a host of other measures, such as permitting no transportation in the PA of people or goods beyond basic necessities, implementing the death penalty against murderers, and razing villages from which attacks are launched. Then as now, such responses have two benefits: First, they send a strong deterrent signal 'Hit us back and we'll hit you back much harder' thereby reducing the number of attacks in the

short term. Second, they impress Palestinians with the Israeli will to survive, and so bring closer their eventual acceptance of the Jewish state.

As Pipes notes, he has been declaring some variation of this argument for many years. It would be a mistake to limit its usage to Pipes and fellow neoconservatives; other commentators recycle its philosophical apparatus in a variety of contexts, often using less inimical and more humanistic language.

Its currency became noticeable upon Ahmadinejad's Columbia appearance. The *Washington Post*'s Anne Applebaum couched American freedoms within a narrative of Iranian ignorance and deprivation: 'Instead of debating freedom of speech in Iran, here we are once again talking about freedom of speech in America, a subject we know a lot more about.' In Applebaum's moral axiom, the United States is disengaged historically from the development of Iranian politics, and so the ready evidence of Iran's functional democracy and its subjection to overt and covert American interference is omitted and thus rendered irrelevant. In turn, the reader is led to question whether Iranians are capable of adequately comprehending freedom without American assistance (which does not appear to preclude military intervention). Applebaum's approach also indicates that flourishes of American self-congratulation are best deployed concurrent with lamentations of Eastern unenlightenment. Such a move shields the commentator from examining the actual state of today's ostensible American freedoms, and simultaneously ushers Iranians into moralistic patrimony, resulting in a type of self-anointed international policing underwritten by erstwhile American mythologies. It would be difficult to quantify, but it is reasonable to speculate that Iranians debate freedom of speech in at least equal numbers to Americans – and they certainly raise these debates with more nuance than do the American op-ed gentry. (It is useful to remember that the non-Persian-speaking Applebaum is making a claim for which she has no qualification to present evidence.)

Jonah Goldberg presented a variation of Applebaum's logic in a commentary for *National Review Online*, speculating that '[i]f the video of Bollinger's statement is distributed throughout the Middle East in general and Iran in particular, it could have a very positive effect. Time will tell.' This speculation is compa- rable to Applebaum's logic because both authors not only seem to accept the sincerity of the United States in its dialogue with Iran, but also sincerely believe that Iranians need that dialogue if they are to ever overcome their premodernity. The crudest example of this sentiment arises in a different framework by liberal cultural critic Carlin Romano, who in summer 2007 published his regular column in the *Chronicle of Higher Educa- tion Review* under the title 'If We Don't Call Them Names, the Terrorists Win.' Romano's argument is straightforward: calling for 'sterner judgment, more forcefully expressed,' he urges politicians and commentators to refer to 'terrorists' – a typically vague, and thus racialized, designation – as 'bastards, lowlife, cowards, scum.' Other options include 'evil' and 'barbarian.'

Romano's argument is troublesome for numerous reasons, but mainly because his contextual understanding of geo- political issues such as Israeli colonization of Palestine and the American invasion of Iraq is morbidly shortsighted and because he fails to make an adequate distinction between so-called terrorists and all Muslims. If followed, then, his recommendation would result in a widespread branding of all Muslim people as 'bastards, lowlife, cowards, scum,' a phenomenon that is anyway already evident. (Were it not, then how could Romano have written his article in the first place? And how could it have been published in the newspaper of record on higher education?) Romano proposes to codify rhetorically the Manichean categories that justify American imperialism and that subordinate Muslims to remarkably violent forms of acculturation into modernity.

But these problems aren't the most noteworthy items in Romano's argument. That distinction belongs to his rationale for name-calling. 'What might we argue in favor of calling terrorists names?' he asks:

> Let's mention just one key goal: the education of the world's Muslim youth. Instead of hearing moral praise and encouragement for terrorism from jihadists, which then gets mixed in their minds with the nonjudgmental, tactical talk of Western officials and media, they'd have to absorb a steady stream of insults of terrorists' intelligence, morality, decency, and reasoning. Young Muslims would have to get used to hearing jihadist heroes described as savages, scum, and uncivilized losers, along with the reasons why. It would intellectually force them, far more than they are forced today, to choose between two visions of the world.

This strategy is preposterous because it reduces the complex socio-political and economic factors that influence terrorism

– in its many forms – to a binaristic moral vision expressed crudely through the use of symbolic naming. Romano believes that effecting a change of vocabulary for an American audience will inspire Muslims to suddenly introspect on their barbarity and then naturally come to realize that submitting themselves to American military and neoliberal domination will resolve all of their problems. (They won't, of course, be clever enough to realize that Romano's recommendation would merely resolve the American problems that inconveniently arise from the choice to cultivate imperialistic fervor.) The strategy also tacitly ascribes a permanent barbarism to Muslims. If it didn't, then Romano would have no basis to conceptualize Muslim youth as so craven and stupid that hearing fellow Muslims being called horrible and dehumanizing names will turn them to the side of those who are so viciously antagonistic.

Romano's argument is an extreme version of a distinct attitude, one shared by Applebaum and Goldberg: Arabs and Muslims, enamored of violence, must be civilized violently.

These approaches are useful to those who are amorous of American civility because they lock Muslims into premodern irrationality. They have the added benefit of shifting attention from expressions of American barbarity: imperialism, torture, the rape and murder of civilians in Iraq, eroded civil rights, neglected human rights. Constricted civil and human rights are of particular concern. In raising this concern, I don't wish to imply that it is new to the United States. There never has been a moment in American history in which civil and human rights were exercised and protected comprehensively; somebody has always been excluded from them at each historical moment, and people have continuously been victim of the corresponding technique of denial-through-sanctimony. The present constriction of civil and human rights is noteworthy because of a few distinctive qualities. In the first place, American government officials have confessed to the use of torture and have proudly restricted what once were legally protected freedoms of privacy and rights to counsel. Moreover, the discourse of justification these days is usually invested in peculiar covenants of security. Those covenants stress the protection of American individuals from terrorism, but circulate from and return to the preservation of state power. The need for protection, however, is often presented as a messianic obligation.

In keeping with these needs it is useful to lecture Ahmadinejad about his supposedly moribund record on civil and human rights. (Ahmadinejad is no champion of justice – see his positions on homosexuality and economic development – but if he were as bad as his simulated representation, then he would be irredeemably debased and imbecilic, rather like George W. Bush in actuality.) This lecturing reaffirms a faux American commitment to civil and human rights that in reality is performed merely at the level of assertion, thereby fulfilling its primary function. In this scenario, Ahmadinejad is a grotesque prop, a necessary bogeyman outfitted with the physical and emotional qualities arising from the not-completely-suppressed psychosis of denial. This type of rhetorical ceremony would be somewhat amusing were it not also malevolent: in so viciously scolding grotesque props like Ahmadinejad, the commentators and intellectuals who invent public opinion not only ignore American civil and human rights abuses, they actually buttress and legitimize them by avoiding introspection through sanctimonious condemnation of the geopolitical (i.e. moral) stranger. Dehumanizing the stranger doesn't merely enable commentators to deny American barbarism; it enables them to facilitate American barbarism through the use of language that renders the stranger an emblem of the entire Muslim World.

One way this totalization is accomplished is through constant attention to the dangers of innate Muslim barbarity. But how do we come to recognize the presence of a threat that is distinctly Muslim? In the world in which human Muslims exist, Islamic symbology is both complex and inconsistent. There are few objects that can accurately represent Islam in its totality. There are no ethnic attributes qualified to do the same. However, in the world in which Muslims are represented by those either invested or complicit in imperialism, terrorism can be reduced to the articulation of visual symbols that signal the threatening presence of Islam. These visual symbols commonly include beards, *kuffiyeh*s, prayer beads, and distinguishing garb (think dirty beige robes and dusty leather sandals).

I don't want to focus on these typical signifiers because other visual symbols have come to stand in for menacing Muslims, and these visual symbols bespeak a more troublesome form of racism and reductionism. The most troublesome of these symbols is the framework of Quranic textuality, Arabic script (in different ways we can see the appropriation into racist symbology of the entire Arabic language, both vocally and aurally). We have reached a point that in American discursive norms all articulations of Islamic culture signify violence, with Arabic script most visibly signifying violent Islamic culture. In the case of Arabic script, we have a linguistic object, or a sound image, morphing into a specific culture signifier; arbiters of popular-culture ethos invest Arabic script with sinister connotations, fomenting something of a semiotic tomfoolery.

The case of Debbie Almontaser is a sensational example of this phenomenon. A Yemeni immigrant and former principal at New York City's public Khalil Gibran International Academy, an Arabic language and culture high school, Almontaser generated controversy when she was asked by a reporter about the phrase 'Intifada NYC,' worn by some members of the organization Arab Women Active in the Arts and Media at one of its sponsored events. Both the event and the organization are unrelated to the Gibran Academy; Almontaser happened to be in attendance. Almontaser explained to the reporter that the slogan is not an endorsement of violence; 'the word basically means "shaking off,"' she noted. Although the term has come to connote suicide bombing in most American media, in reality the first Palestinian intifada was defined by its courageous nonviolent resistance and the second intifada is replete with unreported acts of organized nonviolence. Almontaser was subjected to vicious and factually unsubstantiated attacks by neoconservative media and commentators such as Daniel Pipes, who published articles entitled 'A Madrassa Grows in Brooklyn' and 'Stop the NYC Madrassa' ('madrassa' merely means 'school' in Arabic). The *New York Post* dubbed Almontaser 'the Intifada

Principal' and ran an editorial under the title 'What's Arabic for Shut It Down?' Amid the brouhaha, premeditated and wholly sensationalistic, Randi Weingarten, the president of Almontaser's union, the United Federation of Teachers, took a public stand in opposition to Almontaser, who subsequently resigned and was replaced by the non-Arabic-speaking Danielle Salzberg, 'an ardent Zionist who considered moving to Israel,' according to the *Post*.

There are many lessons to take from these events, among them the knowledge that in moments of crisis the fear and loathing of Arabs will supersede the need to exercise basic civil responsibility. The clear message to the Arab American community is that it cannot undertake any of its own affairs without continuous public scrutiny and external bureaucratic supervision, and can be in any moment profoundly insulted by yet again coming under the authority of Zionist overseers. (I would point out that, if true, Salzberg's affiliation as a Zionist is much more objectionable than anything Almontaser did. Unlike the act of commenting on a T-shirt, Zionism is a clear endorsement of violence. In this case, it is an endorsement of violence against the very students under Salzberg's supervision.) Perhaps the most alarming lesson is the grim realization that freedom of intellectual and cultural expression in the United States will, for the time being, be subordinate to the interests of those who support the aggression of a militarized colonial state in the eastern Mediterranean.

Beyond these lessons we can identify a more interesting phenomenon, that of the semiotic tomfoolery to which I refer above. Nonviolent, workaday Arabic terms come to be stigmatized with murderous, albeit nonsensical, connotations. Anything indicative of Arabic culture – and the attendant being of Arabs themselves – can thereby be viewed as symbolic of a violent presence. Arabs and Muslims cannot signify any sort of cultural existence in the United States without the concomitant potential of irrational belligerence, usually in the form of apolitical terrorism. Other examples support this observation: the ubiquitous charge of 'jihadist' directed at activists and academics supportive of decolonial justice (i.e. Palestinian liberation) who have never spoken of jihad; the harassment of airline passengers carrying Qurans or displaying any sort of Arabic script ('we will not be silent,' for example); the inveterate equation of Islam with fascism; the reduction of all forms of Palestinian resistance to terrorism; the conceptualization of hijab as emblematic of helplessness and oppression.

Perhaps these examples are all exemplified by the poster students found emblazoned across George Washington University's campus one morning in the lead-up to the David Horowitz-sponsored 'Islamo-fascism Awareness Week.' Depicting what appeared to be an Arab wearing a suicide-bomb vest and toting an AK-47, the poster described the figure as the 'typical Muslim.' This image likely entered many people's minds when Mahmoud Ahmadinejad stepped in front of a microphone at genteel Columbia University. Eventually, a group of seven GWU students confessed to having posted the fliers, along with others that read 'Do You Hate Muslims? So Do We!!!' claiming that the messages were intended to be satirical. This admission, which we have no reason to doubt, was generally overlooked by the many groups and commentators who condemned the posters, presumably because acknowledging their satirical intent might have undermined the goal of raising awareness about and condemning the very real Islamophobia plaguing college campuses and the United States more broadly.

We can accomplish these goals more effectively by exploring the situation in its entirety, because even if the posters were satire it doesn't alter or undermine the tropological factors that allow them to be satirically effective – that is, to be recognized as representations of a distinct outlook typified by a particular symbology. I would argue that the posters can identify the negative imagery of Islamophobia even more profoundly as satire than they would have as a literal pronouncement. How is this possible? We should keep in mind that the posters weren't actually recognized as satire, a remarkably telling fact. Their believability despite their excessive racism and caricatured portrayal of a fetishized enemy bespeaks a mainstreaming of Islamophobia that enables its visions of Muslim violence to become normative. It is precisely because of the existence of Islamophobia in the United States that people could read this type of exaggerated imagery as completely realistic. The satire didn't work despite its heavy-handedness because it wasn't able to separate itself adequately from what it endeavored to ridicule.

I could wear a shirt that proclaims, in Arabic, 'I love America,' or some other pithily patriotic sentiment, and end up in prison. Sadly, I do not exaggerate. Such a shirt could literally land me in prison. This irony would be funny – just as the GWU students' satire could have been funny – if not for the fact that it emblematizes a different sort of political reality: a nation sick with an unwillingness to question the representational dogmas borne of imperialistic desire, and one that has no ability to express a single form of patriotic sentiment that isn't also latently racist. I would enact this point by becoming a threatening patriot, but I have no desire to invite this national sickness to unfold on my own healthy body. Besides, Mahmoud Ahmadinejad has already unwittingly enacted this point for all of us.

Where does this process begin? In what conditions, in other words, does an ethnic symbology incubate and then become a widely accepted negative representation?

It is difficult to answer these questions with precision because the dissemination of ethnic imagery is complex and never fully constant. That imagery circulates through different, sometimes competing, levels of society and evolves continually based on encounters with different forms of power. Yet the metonymical qualities of Islam as a catalyst of imagined violence are largely consistent on both the left and the right in the United States. And we do know that the process is never random or accidental. Or, put differently, had Ahmadinejad been the repressive Shah of Iran rather than the repressive president of an enemy country, he would have been welcomed effulgently by corporate media and by Lee Bollinger. Bollinger would have merely executed a different sort of grandstanding, this one unabashedly effusive, but performed in the service of the exact same cause.

The zealots of clandestine faith

A theism is inherently paradoxical. The act of naming unbelief is fundamentally doctrinal. That is to say, in its most sincere incarnation unbelief is deeply personal, but when unbelief is labeled and categorized it becomes something communal. This is the point at which atheism encounters problems, when it evolves from a personal outlook into a public idea.

Vocal atheism is also problematic because to expound on atheism requires the atheist to profess. Atheism, in other words, works best as a world-view or philosophy that precedes identification. Atheists do not believe in the existence of God and generally oppose the religions that grow from the desire to worship. There is much to admire in people willing to question the sacred and the consecrated, which are supposed to be impervious to mockery or opprobrium, an unfortunate ethic that warrants reconsideration. The problem is that in certain conditions atheism assumes the same structure it rightly criticizes in religion.

Atheism needn't be described merely as unbelief. It is a belief in the nonexistence of God, although it's difficult to articulate belief in a negative. Beyond the basic question of God, though, atheists adhere to various forms of belief, some of them theological and all of them political. Those who do not believe in the existence of God are remarkably diverse in moral and philosophical world-view. They shouldn't be reduced merely to skeptics.

My goal in this essay isn't to extrapolate on the rightness or wrongness of the proposition that there is no God. In a sense, I don't much care. Belief or unbelief in God is a personal affair – at least it should be. To me, anyway, it is a personal affair, and it's not a question I find of particular value in thinking about the nuances of the world. Let me put it this way: if we could in this moment prove or disprove the existence of God (and we can't – and we never can), I fail to see how the current state of the world would be permanently altered. People would still be hungry because, God or not, the fortunate have no intention of sharing their disproportionate wealth. People would still fight wars because in the end God can rationalize or mobilize a war, but few wars are actually fought over competing deities – they are fought over land, power, resources, and other objects of upper-class covetousness. Without God, people would be just as stupid as atheists claim that religion makes us.

Many atheists blame belief in God for creating the conditions that enable or nurture atrocities such as dispossession and genocide. They are partly correct, but not fully correct because they are too optimistic. In reality, if God weren't around to justify human participation in injustice, humans wouldn't take long to find a capable stand-in.

Given my indifference to the basic question of God, I don't want to enter into a theological or philosophical discussion of God as physical reality or metaphysical abstraction. I am both unqualified for and uninterested in this sort of discussion. I am more interested in the cultural meanings of the recent upsurge of book-length atheist manifestos, particularly in the context of some of the other pressing issues in the United States. We are seeing now what might be called an atheist movement. In what conditions has this movement arisen? And what, as represented by the latest books promoting atheism, is today's atheist movement engaged with morally and politically?

I'm thinking particularly of three books: Sam Harris's *Letter to a Christian Nation*, Richard Dawkins's *The God Delusion*, and Christopher Hitchens's *God Is Not Great*. All three books are bestsellers, written by people well known for other pursuits – that is to say, by people whose intellectual qualifications are comprehensive. None of these authors is a dilettante or a mere polemicist. All of them, however, managed to write sloppy and loathsome books.

These books, which don't define the new atheist movement but certainly epitomize it, are arrant signs of their time. If, as the authors claim, religion has ushered into the world unmitigated irrationality and intolerance, then the authors unwittingly prove it by enacting that claim. They employ rhetoric exemplifying precisely what they condemn. (Harris: 'There are millions – maybe hundreds of millions – of Muslims who would be willing to die before they would allow your version of compassion to gain a foothold on the Arabian Peninsula' (88); 'Throughout Europe, Muslim communities often show little inclination to acquire the secular and civil values of their host countries, and yet they exploit these values to the utmost, demanding tolerance for their misogyny, their anti-Semitism, and the religious hatred that is regularly preached in their mosques' (84); 'The problem with religion – as with Nazism, Stalinism, or any other totalitarian mythology – is the problem of dogma itself' (43).) The only real value to *Letter to a Christian Nation*, *The God Delusion*, and *God Is Not Great* is their fantastic illumination of how being religious sometimes has nothing to do with religion. They also illuminate the fact that dogmatism isn't indivisible from devotion, or that devotion isn't confined to theistic relationships.

I am highly sympathetic to productive critiques of religious perfidy, of which there is plenty around the world; this unfortunate abundance is the only truly ecumenical feature of religion. Organized religion produces or is complicit in all kinds of awful things and contributes its fair share of senselessness to the world, but I find it equally senseless to attack religion by reproducing its magisterial tendencies. The greatest benefit to criticizing religion is not the presumption of having disproved God, but the value of avoiding deference and obedience and promulgating an ethics of analytical independence. Challenging religion is most useful when it encourages us to think for ourselves rather than recapitulating what textual authority tells us to think; avoiding recapitulation makes us less manipulable as social and political agents. Based on their rhetorical effrontery, it appears that Harris, Dawkins, and Hitchens want to replace religion with their own rational enlightenment, an unstated but unmistakable bartering of authority.

Dawkins, for instance, boasts, 'Being an atheist is nothing to be apologetic about. On the contrary, it is something to be proud of, standing tall to face the far horizon, for atheism nearly always indicates a healthy independence of mind and, indeed, a healthy mind' (3). Hitchens echoes this sentiment, suggesting that '[w]e atheists do not require any priests, or any hierarchy above us, to police our doctrine. Sacrifices and ceremonies are abhorrent to us, as are relics and the worship of any images or objects (even including objects in the form of one man's most useful innovation: the bound book)' (6). Harris speaks directly to his imagined reader: 'I would like to acknowledge that there are many points on which you and I agree. We agree, for instance, that if one of us is right, the other is wrong' (3).

These arguments are typically arrogant and simplistic. They exemplify a theme common throughout the three books: atheists are smarter, healthier, and more adjusted than religious folk. Yet this point is so poorly argued that even religious cretins can expose its foolishness. Positing that atheists are almost always mentally healthy is precisely as demonstrable as the notion that education makes people morally better. As to Hitchens, he hasn't so much made a statement as he has put forth a non sequitur. I am an Orthodox Christian, by culture at least. I don't require anybody to police my doctrine, either. Neither is it the case that sacrifices and ceremonies necessarily are conducted in the service of God. Most ceremonies, I would guess, are conducted to some other end. It is difficult to respond seriously to Harris's passage. He spends his entire book arguing vehemently that his position is exclusively correct, but nevertheless has the generosity to offer up two options: agree with everything he says or be wrong. Perhaps Dawkins had Harris subconsciously in mind when he came up with the phrase 'the God delusion.'

I'm not interested in responding to the new atheists by merely impugning their motivations as they are exposed through various rhetorical choices. It would be more useful to historicize this new atheism. It's not an accident, for example, that the rise of atheism in the literary and intellectual marketplace comes at a moment of pronounced Islamophobia in the West. Harris, Dawkins, and Hitchens lambaste all religions; they are consistent in their belief that religion *ipso facto* is problematic and best abolished. Islamophobia, however, has influenced the marketplace in which their works have become bestsellers. And it is in the context of Islamophobia that atheism becomes most appealing and persuasive.

The authors aren't completely disinterested in their condemnation of religion; they invoke Islam in moments that are supposed to be rhetorically vital. Hitchens has infamously highlighted what he deems Muslim backwardness, and in *The God Delusion* Dawkins writes, 'One of the unhappiest spectacles to be seen on our streets today is the image of a woman swathed in shapeless black from head to toe, peering out at the world through a tiny slit. The burka is not just an instrument of oppression of women and claustral repression of their liberty and beauty; not just a token of egregious male cruelty and tragically cowed female submission' (362); the slit in the burka, Dawkins goes on to theorize, is metaphorical of the freedom that atheism promises. Harris, for his part, has described Islam as 'the most pungent' religion.

It wouldn't be fair to argue that the new atheist movement is a by-product of Islamophobia, but Islamophobia provides much of the context for the books and for the culture that responds to them. The new atheism is therefore partly reliant on Islamophobia, which arises primarily from a colonialist binary of modernity and premodernity, a temporal structure that Harris, Dawkins, and Hitchens reproduce to render atheism normatively civilized. Islam becomes atheism's quintessential Other. If anything has turned Westerners away from trust of religion, it is the strange and violent Islam presented incessantly to them in cultural and geopolitical analysis, a perception that Harris, Dawkins, and Hitchens attempt to validate and then exploit.

Take this example from Harris, who understands the value of Islamophobia to his imagined Christian reader:

Why don't you lose any sleep over whether to convert to Islam? Can you prove that Allah is not the one, true God? Can you prove that the archangel Gabriel did not visit Muhammad in his cave? Of course not. But you need not prove any of these things to reject the beliefs of Muslims as absurd. The burden is upon them to prove that their beliefs about God and Muhammad are valid. They have not done this. They cannot do this. Muslims are simply not making claims about reality that can be corroborated. This is perfectly apparent to anyone who has not anesthetized himself with the dogma of Islam.

The truth is, you know exactly what it is like to be an atheist with respect to the beliefs of Muslims. Isn't it obvious that Muslims are fooling themselves? Isn't it obvious that anyone who thinks the Koran is the perfect word of the creator of the universe has not read the book critically? Isn't it obvious that the doctrine of Islam represents a near-perfect barrier to honest inquiry? Yes, these things are obvious. (7)

Correspondingly, the new atheism, as presented by its public intellectuals, belongs to the realm of white male hauteur. The form of atheism that Harris, Dawkins, and Hitchens promote is remarkably smug and Eurocentric. (Dawkins wants atheists to be called 'brights,' an idea that Hitchens admits is conceited.) The logic of their atheism is basically a repossessed Enlightenment ethos outfitted for contemporary paradigms vis-à-vis modern geopolitical circumstances. None of the writers does a good job of exploring his own historical rootedness, resulting in a glaring methodological vacuum. The methodology they do employ is markedly provincial and ignores the abundance of philosophical analysis of religion arising from Indigenous, postcolonial, and Eastern communities. In the absence of adequate treatment of these sources and traditions, Harris, Dawkins, and Hitchens betray one of their main rhetorical flaws: overconfidence in the probity of Western Enlightenment rationalism. (A much more satisfying exploration of politics and religion can be found in David Hurst Thomas's *Skull Wars*.)

Unsurprisingly, in this framework atheism often substitutes for tacit racism – or at least racism tacitly affixes itself to an intellectual apparatus enamored of its supposedly objective rationality. The idea that Harris, Dawkins, and Hitchens advance relies on the unquestioned superiority of Western science and its purportedly moral infallibility. All three writers gleefully recount the complicity of religion in oppression but ignore the sins of Western science, which include participation in the Nazi Holocaust, the phrenological justification for chattel slavery, and centuries of injustice against Indians. Western science, not religion, invented and legitimized modern racism, although religion is profoundly complicit. The authors discount traditional ways of knowing – which tend to be abstractly 'religious,' though not quite in Western usage – as useless superstition. They reduce the voluminous history of Islamic theology to the realm of madmen. They haughtily dismiss the complex interrelation of religious observation with poverty and oppression. There are more than 6 billion people of faith in the world; each of these people has a unique relationship with a deity or set of deities, and each adheres to a different level of worship. According to Harris, Dawkins, and Hitchens, though, all people of faith are fundamentally the same. No Holy Book could possibly be this reductive.

One can almost picture each author ruminating on a cloud of velvety transcendence, index finger to chin, vertical wrinkle dividing furrowed brows, cloaked in the stately white vestments of intellectual perfection, putting the final touches on his magnificent thesis: Western science, good; religion, bad.

Each author is certain that science is metaphorical shit that don't stink. But let's be honest: science has merely confirmed much of what the Quran already said about the workings of the natural world; in North America, science was a few millennia behind what Indigenous peoples, through belief systems, already knew about human anatomy and local ecosystems. How has science been getting on with the environment these days, by the way?

There are countless good things to be said about science, and in it we can uncover all kinds of important solutions to serious problems. A society that values belief and faith over science is one that is bound to become repressive. Religion should never make policy; good science should. My point is not to disparage science. My point is that one could reduce science to exactly what Harris, Dawkins, and Hitchens reduce religion to, using the same methodology. Hence what is most objectionable about their methodologies, the fact that they cherry-pick evidence to support a wildly reductive thesis. The most disturbing aspect of this thesis is its use of dogmatic and racist discourses that render the philosophical apparatus of atheism coterminous with the features of religion to which it so adamantly objects.

There is absolutely no precedent to suggest that abandoning religion and adhering to science will make humans any less apt to commit injustice or act irrationally. The adamantly pro-war Hitchens, who continues to champion the disastrous American invasion of Iraq, is clear evidence of this fact. And if atheism makes people more rational, then how is it possible that Hitchens became one of its spokespersons? His political stances undermine his core thesis about religion.

There is plenty of evidence, in fact, to suggest that engagement with traditional Indigenous beliefs often results in a more responsible human being. It bears pointing out, in any case, that some of the world's nastiest regimes have been nominally secular (if not completely unreligious): Britain during Empire, Israel, colonial France, Nazi Germany, corporate America.

Another troubling feature of this new atheism exists in *The God Delusion*. Dawkins questions why atheists have such large numbers and so little political influence: 'The status of atheists in America today is on a par with that of homosexuals fifty years ago' (4). He concludes that because atheists are so independent-minded and nonconformist it's difficult to organize them: 'Indeed, organizing atheists has been compared to herding cats, because they tend to think independently and will not conform to authority' (4). I would suggest that herding atheists is difficult because atheism doesn't lend itself to the sort of political organizing that Dawkins envisions. He wants atheists to lobby as a political bloc with a set of interests, but the moment he put forth this proposal atheism became scarcely distinguishable from the Baptist and Jewish groups on Capitol Hill. It became a collective that God manages to usher into political action. Dawkins's version of atheism is just another religion.

At one point Dawkins even proselytizes, without a hint of irony: 'If this book works as I intend, religious readers who open it will be atheists when they put it down' (5).

Zealots of clandestine faith

In the introduction to *God Is Not Great*, Hitchens explains that one of the four main atheist objections to religion is that 'it manages to combine the maximum of servility with the maximum of solipsism' (4). I agree with the essence of Hitchens's argument. We should attack anything that encourages lethargy or apathy in humans, and religion often is guilty of encouraging both. (By leaving things 'in God's hands,' for example, the faithful can forestall the abrogation of injustices that are humanly correctible.) However, I don't see how one can rightly switch religion with atheism as a viable corrective. All kinds of secular institutions induce political lethargy and apathy: corporate media, secondary and post-secondary education, entertainment, sports, and, according to Hitchens's perturbed colleague Richard Dawkins, atheism. The problem of engagement is not purely a religious one; it is a comprehensive problem that requires an attention much more serious than the one Hitchens devotes to it.

A final problem with the new atheism is illuminated throughout *Letter to a Christian Nation*. At the start of the book, Harris notes, 'Although [Christian] liberals and moderates do not fly planes into buildings or organize their lives around apocalyptic prophecy, they rarely question the legitimacy of raising a child to believe that she is a Christian, a Muslim, or a Jew' (ix). Harris is troubled by upbringing, repeating this objection at the end of the book: 'Only [after discovering the nature of reality] will the practice of raising our children to believe that they are Christian, Muslim, or Jewish be widely recognized as the ludicrous obscenity that it is' (88). Here Harris renders religion exclusively scriptural, which is a spectacularly narrow understanding of Christianity, Islam, and Judaism, and of religion in general. He ignores religion as a cultural apparatus, one that cannot simply be eliminated or overcome.

There are plenty of Jews who never set foot in Temple but who are proudly Jewish culturally. Asking Jewish parents not to raise their children as Jews is like asking African American parents not to raise their children Black. I am an indigenous Christian by culture, and, even if I never send my children to church, I will impart to them what it means to have a lineage in this identification. It is what will tie them into their ancestral culture and create relationships with those who preceded them. White Eurocentrists like Harris haven't the slightest understanding of what it means to belong to something communally meaningful and culturally beautiful, something that invests itself into world-view and body language, into voice and relation, into the essence of who we are at our simplest but most complex, a something that can only be experienced because it can't properly be described if it is detached from its everyday practice. I'm speaking of the vivacity and artistry of a communal history that makes me everything I am or want to be. All people rooted in ancient, substantive non-Western histories know exactly what I mean; few of them would ever dream of trading in who they are for something as boring and unbending as Western atheism. Harris relies on cold logic in the absence of a soulful existence. If Harris claims anything other than an intensely vanilla subsistence, he fails to illustrate it anywhere in his book.

Harris also views religious teaching simplistically. Religious teaching, for instance, is the cornerstone of Indigenous cultures, the very phenomenon that renders them distinct. Asking them to give up their cultures, something Harris does by insisting that humans abandon all forms of belief and worship, has proved time and again to be a horrible idea, one that nearly all scholars and policymakers recognize as deeply immoral. And nobody can rightly blame the ills of the world on Indigenous peoples. If Harris were to succeed in transforming Indians into everyday atheists they would disappear soon thereafter. Harris essentially advocates voluntary ethnic cleansing of those to whom the practice of belief is indivisible from peoplehood.

Harris's presentation of atheism is consummately pedestrian, but that's not its biggest problem; the way Harris wants atheism to be practiced is implicitly violent.

Dawkins and Hitchens suffer from the same moral atrophy. If we were to pursue atheism according to their blueprint (and they present us with no other choice), then we'd all become vainglorious white men with inordinate privilege who whine about the discrimination we experience. If we retain our own identities as either religious or spiritual beings, to any degree, we'll be wrong. All of us. Because religion, of course, is inflexible and dogmatic.

Although Harris, Dawkins, and Hitchens failed badly in their attempts, it would be useful for somebody to write a solid contemporary book on atheism. Even so, I'm not entirely sure that it's a good idea. The more that atheism becomes textually institutionalized the more it resembles a religion. Its uniqueness and value lie in its natural absence of uniformity, not in its ability to be presented cohesively. Not to believe in God is a perfectly reasonable proposition, and one can take up this proposition in the service of a happy and productive life. But the problem isn't God Himself (or itself, depending on your point of view); the problem is the institutionalization of God into religious, textual, social, and political systems. If we institutionalize the non-God into these systems, then we won't have averted the problem of religion; we will have reproduced it.

Harris, Dawkins, and Hitchens represent only a few versions of atheism, not atheism itself, which is good for both atheists and believers. In the end, their books comprise uninspiring polemics delivered through fallacious rhetoric. If the logic they present awaits us, then I'm not too hopeful about that glorious day when religion is supposed to become obsolete, replaced by things that claim to be more rational and compassionate. The question of the existence or nonexistence of God matters even less now, because, as Harris, Dawkins, and Hitchens have demonstrated, in a world without God stupidity will still be alive and well.

Conclusion

We live in a world in which a decorated feminist of the American left can characterize the 'Iraqi resistance' – as if it is one thing – as an unvarying collective of hideous evildoers. She characterizes the Iraqi resistance in the singular because her usage renders it coterminous with all Iraqi people. Reacting to a suggestion by Alexander Cockburn that progressives show more solidarity with the Iraqi resistance, this sapient author wonders, 'With whom, exactly, are we supposed to be showing solidarity? Al Qaeda in Mesopotamia? Shiites massacring their Sunni neighbors? Sunnis killing Shiites? Religious reactionaries who have murdered doctors, professors, working women, Christians, students, hand-holding couples?'

Her sarcasm functions only to reinforce the fact that some white Americans, including liberal feminists, have a hellish time identifying with Arabs, or even identifying them as human: 'So, okay, call me ignorant: The Iraqi resistance isn't dominated by theocrats, ethnic nationalists, die-hard Baathists, jihadis, kidnappers, beheaders and thugs?'

Unforgivably romanticized Christians are easier to get on with: 'The [Nicaraguan] Sandinistas and the [Salvadoran] FMLN were far from perfect, but they were leftists. They stood for health care, education, land distribution, modernization – not burning down liquor stores and music shops, beating up unveiled women, suicide-bombing ordinary civilians, bringing back sharia law.' This disparity explains why liberals held potluck dinners in support of the Sandinistas and the FMLN; indeed, '[i]f the Central American revolutionaries had resisted American intervention in the name of the Spanish Inquisition and spent a lot of time ethnically cleansing their neighborhoods, American leftists probably wouldn't have been so eager to hold potluck suppers for them.'

With this piece, Katha Pollitt has transformed herself into a type of writer she is supposed to detest. She is to Arabs what Rush Limbaugh is to women: she generalizes with a smug and condescending tone and her discourse evinces the sort of certitude that only wrongness can produce. Feminism, Pollitt's rhetorical identity, is a movement for justice; because she circumscribes justice by outfitting feminism with racism, Pollitt transformed her feminism into stock hypocrisy. Pollitt, after all, misses her own point: we should be showing solidarity with the 'doctors, professors, working women, Christians, students, hand-holding couples' – in other words, the Iraqis. She makes it sound as if identifying with Iraqi resistance limits us to al-Qaeda and sectarian agitators, yet there are millions of progressive and workaday Iraqis resisting in creative ways. But Pollitt reduces all Iraqis unhappy with military occupation to terrorists and thugs.

The whole thing makes me feel uncultured. Becoming uncultured is what happens in the United States if one insists that Arabs aren't barbarians. Arabs are supposed to be what the white left wants us to be. It doesn't matter that the white left knows nothing about us; it knows enough to know that a proper world can only exist in its own image, and so knowledge of self supersedes knowledge that is intercultural or comprehensive. And knowledge of self, of course, is transmitted directly from (an exuberantly secular) heaven.

We live in a world in which lots of perspectives are amiss. Today, though, the most vexing challenge we face is developing productive inter-communal dialogue. It is easy to locate this conclusion if one identifies as Arab, because there are few spaces on the left or right of the United States in which our diverse viewpoints are taken seriously, much less welcomed. We hope that a productive dialogue – adding the adjective 'productive' intimates that we will actually be listened to – can initiate a process of coming together around different cultures based on the assumption that no one of those cultures need be controlling or normative.

I want to think about this desire in the context of Pollitt's comments because the most troublesome dimension of her article is its reduction of all Iraqis to the worst elements of resistance to American genocide. She evokes prototypically racist assumptions about Arab violence as natural inclination, fine-tuning the point by raising it from within a framework that conceptualizes Arabs as indelibly premodern. Pollitt also highlights Iraqi savagery by comparing it to Central American revolution, which she deems more savory to liberal sensibilities. (This move assumes that the point of struggle among oppressed peoples around the world is to please fastidious white liberals, which sums up the entire problem of white liberalism.) She thereby justifies selective empathy by ushering suffering humans into disparate moral categories, those occupying the upper regions of white approval worthy of a potluck dinner.

This rationale is specious morally. It also is intellectually sophistic. Very few white leftists, then or now, have held potlucks in support of the Palestinians, long facing vicious ethnic cleansing, a situation at least as drastic as Central America's faux socialist revolutions (which often replace horrible political systems with renamed horrible political systems). During the first intifada of 1987–1990, for instance, the Palestinians engaged largely in nonviolent resistance. The town of Beit Sahour was even nominated for a Nobel Peace Prize for its creative and resilient civil disobedience amid Israeli brutality, which included breaking children's bones, an award it undoubtedly should have won, and would have won had American and European liberals given a damn. The Palestinians didn't fit a single one of Pollitt's characterizations of Iraqi resistance (reductive as they are), and so Pollitt can't raise the same objections to explain the silence on the American left around Palestinians; indeed, they would have been the model recipients of Western liberal support according to the criteria Pollitt articulates. Nor did white leftists ever hold potlucks for Kurds, who have been victims of Arab Iraqi perfidy. I'm still waiting to be invited to a potluck in support of the Lebanese victims of Israel's 2006 invasion.

(In any case, these potlucks on behalf of foreign political movements are almost always useless disport, a way to materially articulate self-satisfied complaisance passing itself off as authentic solidarity.)

Let's forget about potlucks. The sad and simple fact is that most white liberals have a remarkably difficult time identifying sincerely with the subjects of their sympathy. This is especially true when those subjects are Arab or Muslim. Pollitt's article illuminates what that difficultly looks like when it appears as political analysis. It's much easier to reduce strangers to their most sensationalistic actions than to take the time it requires to understand who they are in all their variance and complexity.

For this reason, I am eager to find ways to initiate productive dialogue around multifarious issues in various locations. We live in a world in which a decorated feminist of the American left can argue through blatant racism because few people investigate who others are beyond the certitude of deterministic cultural knowledge. With Arabs, this problem is acute because we exist in political colloquy as characters, never narrators. We are not perfect; we are not even particularly special. But we aren't what those on both the left and the right have made us out to be. We too deserve the courtesy of telling our own cultural and historical stories. Why would we not want to exercise this basic courtesy? We certainly don't want folks like Michael Moore and Katha Pollitt to narrate our identity. And these are folks who are supposed to be on the side of goodness and clear thinking.

The point is not to persuade or to coerce, but to access the intrinsic satisfaction that accrues from having the power to speak and be heard. In terms of pragmatic goals, we will want to create a set of elemental assumptions about Arabs and Muslims different from the ones currently in existence. This goal will come to fruition only through the willingness of others actually to listen and to consider the possibility that Arabs aren't necessarily what others have already decided we are.

Please disagree with me; please argue with me; please point out where I am wrong; but please don't be so damn certain from the outset that I represent a culture or world-view that is fundamentally inferior.

Every group, ethnic or political, is adamant that it be listened to and represented accurately. Fine. This desire is reasonable as both moral proposition and political strategy. But the desire needs to be extended: it needs to be practiced and not merely demanded. On this front, white liberals are the guiltiest demographic – that is to say, the most hypocritical. Their counterparts, neoconservatives, don't even pretend that they like anybody else, which renders them odious but not sanctimonious.

The culture wars are at base a by-product of sanctimony usurping praxis. Their primary result has been the abrogation of common points of dialogue. The uncultured wars, I hope,